What people are sa

"*Walk This Way* is an excellent
riches of the Christian faith. ".
familiar words we may have heard many times before but ne-
er really thought about, and this book unpacks them with clarity and grace. I heartily recommend it for everyone looking into
Confirmation and for anyone wanting a refresher in the foundations of what we believe."   **Rod Thomas,**
Bishop of Maidstone.

"This is an excellent book. It will help establish new believers
in the faith, refresh longstanding saints in the truths of God's
Word, guide those who are being trained for various minis-
tries in the church and be a valuable resource for clergy and
other leaders who are training them. I pray that it will be well
used across the world, and especially among Anglicans."

Andrew Cheah,
Dean of St Mary's Cathedral, Kuala Lumpur.

"In the world today there is an urgent need for good, basic teaching on the essentials of the Christian faith. This book makes a
big contribution towards meeting this need. Its various sections
give a commentary, discussion questions and prayer suggestions.
It will be of value to young and old, and especially to confirmation and youth groups."

Ben Kwashi,
Bishop of Jos and General Secretary of GAFCON.

'Be strong in the Lord and in the strength of his might' - Eph 6:10.

WALK THIS WAY

to Robert

for your confirmation

Sept 2021

Guided reflections on Christian faith, life, and prayer for individuals and groups.

By

Ash Carter, Ros Clarke, and Lee Gatiss

Walk This Way
Guided reflections on Christian faith, life, and prayer for individuals and groups.

© Church Society/Lost Coin Books 2020.

Published for Church Society by Lost Coin Books, London.
email: lostcoinbooks@gmail.com
web: www.lostcoinbooks.com

Church Society
Ground Floor, Centre Block
Hille Business Estate, 132 St Albans Road
Watford WD24 4AE, UK
Tel +44 (0)1923 255410
www.churchsociety.org
admin@churchsociety.org

Church Society

EQUIPPING GOD'S
PEOPLE TO LIVE
GOD'S WORD

LOST C●IN

ISBN: 9781999327057

Printed in the UK

Contents

Preface

Walking through the countryside can be a perilous undertaking, especially if you don't like mud. For those of us who are used to flat pavements and maps on our phones, it can be a hazardous and anxious enterprise. It's so easy to get lost or confused! How much better it is, however, when some kind souls have beaten down paths ahead of us in the grass, or left helpful signposts along the way to show us where to go.

The Christian life is often described in the Bible as a walk. The Bible is our Ordnance Survey map, with detailed instructions and all that we need to find our route (if we figure out how to use it properly). For many centuries, people have got their bearings and begun learning to follow that map with guidance from the Apostles' Creed, the Ten Commandments, and the Lord's Prayer. These texts are often literally written on the walls of many churches, as a reminder of their central importance as simpler signposts along the way. Billions of people have been baptised into the faith, regularly attended church, and celebrated the Lord's Supper, but they haven't always understood what they are all about. If you need help to really get going or inspiration to continue on your own adventure of faith as a Christian, this book is for you. It takes a careful look at those major roads and signposts, and tries to light the path ahead with clarity and grace.

We have divided the Creed, the Commandments, and the Lord's Prayer into bite-sized portions to make it easier to digest what they are teaching, one step at a time. With questions to ponder and prayers to pray, this is an ideal way to spend a few minutes each day on your own, or an hour a week in a group with friends perhaps, thinking about the key elements of classic Christianity.

Following these 33 short chapters are 3 slightly longer ones, looking at baptism, the Lord's Supper, and the church. These are like more substantial picnic meals along the journey, designed to be read in one go and to give you the big picture on these important subjects, without being too heavy. Finally, we have added a classic question-and-answer catechism, which unpacks some of the key doctrines of the faith in an easily accessible conversational format, that you could use at church or with a friend, to cheer you on your way.

We hope you will enjoy your trek through this book, and pray that it will help you follow Jesus—the way, the truth, and the life.

ASH CARTER

ROS CLARKE

LEE GATISS

Contributors

Ash Carter is the Rector of Kirk Ella (St Andrew) and Willerby in Hull, and co-author of *God Speaks: Listening, Connecting, Relating*.

Ros Clarke is the Associate Director of Church Society and Course Leader of the Priscilla Programme, an online training course for women.

Lee Gatiss is the Director of Church Society and editor of *Foundations of Faith: Reflections on the Thirty-nine Articles*.

The Apostles' Creed

I believe in God, the Father Almighty,

Creator of heaven and earth.

I believe in Jesus Christ, his only Son our Lord.

He was conceived by the Holy Spirit

and born of the virgin Mary.

He suffered under Pontius Pilate,

was crucified, died, and was buried.

He descended to the dead.

On the third day he rose again.

He ascended into heaven and sits at the right hand of the Father.

From there he shall come again to judge the living and the dead.

I believe in the Holy Spirit, the holy catholic church,

the communion of saints, the forgiveness of sins,

the resurrection of the body, and the life everlasting.

Amen.

The Apostles' Creed from

An English Prayer Book

A Revolutionary Act

To say the Creed is a counter-cultural, revolutionary act. To some it may appear mundane, merely reciting some old words in a church along with others in the congregation. But what we are doing when we join in this public profession of faith is taking a stand against all that is evil in this world.

The history of the Creed

The Apostles' Creed has been a part of Christian worship since the early church. It probably started life as a declaration of faith designed for those being baptised as new believers. It sums up, in just over 100 easily-memorised words, some essential Christian teachings. It tells us about the God we believe in—Father, Son, and Holy Spirit. It recounts the past, present, and future of the story of our salvation. And it briefly highlights the blessings we enjoy as believers, giving us a trustworthy summary of the faith as it has been passed down to us through the centuries from the very earliest witnesses.

It was not, as far as we know, actually written by the Apostles, Jesus's inner circle of 12 disciples. But as it captures some crucial points from the Gospels and the earliest preaching of the good news, it came to be called the Apostles' Creed. A slightly longer version, with more detail and clarity on certain points, was approved by the Council of Nicea in the year 325, and is known as the Nicene Creed. Another creed focusing in detail on the doctrine of the Trinity came to be associated with the early church leader Athanasius, and is called the Athanasian Creed.

The Apostles' Creed has been included in Anglican services since the first *Book of Common Prayer* in English, in the sixteenth century. Before that it was recited all over Europe in Latin; the first word is *Credo*, which means "I believe", and so it became known in English as the Creed. The *Thirty-nine Articles*, the Church of England's official confession of faith, says that "The Three Creeds, Nicene Creed, Athanasius's Creed, and that which is commonly called the Apostles' Creed, ought thoroughly to be received and believed: for they may be proved by most certain warrants of holy Scripture."

Taking a stand

In many places, Christians literally stand to say these words every Sunday. Because they are not just a pithy summary of biblical doctrine on certain key points, and a reassuring reminder of the story of our redemption; they are also a statement of personal commitment: here I stand. Yes, me too. I believe.

It may get me into trouble—but I believe. My faith is not a private hobby or a game of personal "let's pretend"—but I say out loud, I believe. It may attract unwanted attention—but I believe. My generation and many around me do not—but I believe. I don't believe in "me" or the flimsy gods and human idols of this world— I believe in *this* God. I didn't just make it up myself—but I believe this Creed.

It is important to be able to say the Creed for ourselves, with feeling and understanding, from our hearts as well as our heads. It would be possible simply to say it by rote because our parents or our friends at church do so, but it is meant to be a joyful statement of something deep in our own souls. Just because they are words said by millions of Christians through the centuries does not mean they cannot be my words too.

Many people reject or ignore the past because they think everything must be so much better in our day and age. So it is no small thing to express solidarity with Christians throughout the generations, and across the world, by declaring that we believe these universal, timeless truths taken from God's word.

By adding our voices to theirs, we join the revolution. We take a stand against the godless culture around us, and the ungodliness within us, which is in rebellion against King Jesus. It's a stick in the eye of the devil, who would prefer that we didn't know or say the Creed with conviction.

Yes, saying the Creed is one of the most radical things you could ever do.

Questions for Reflection

1. Why would it be a good idea to memorise the Creed?

2. Do you agree that the things taught in the Creed can be proved from holy Scripture?

3. What questions do you have about parts of the Creed, on which you are hoping to get clearer?

Prayer

Almighty God,
whose Son Jesus Christ is the way, the truth, and the life:
By the power of your Spirit,
enable us to stand firm in the faith we are taught by your word,
with courage and clarity all the days of our lives.
In Jesus's name,
Amen.

A Declaration of Dependence

I believe in God, the Father Almighty

"I will be a Father to you, and you will be my sons and daughters, says the Lord Almighty."

2 Corinthians 6:18

If you type "I believe" into Google, it helpfully suggests various ways to complete that sentence. "I believe I can fly" is the top suggestion, closely followed by belief in Father Christmas, miracles, and love. Magic, ghosts, unicorns, and angels are not far from the top either. Is this what belief is, in the twenty-first century—a yearning, a wish, for anything beyond the ordinary, something which may even be entirely fictional? And does that matter, as long as it gives me a warm, happy glow to believe it?

A declaration of dependence

The first line of the Apostles' Creed is not an expression of wishful thinking. Rather, it is a declaration of dependence on the God who is truly there. It says I believe in God—not in myself and my abilities. I don't believe in chance or fate or the blind forces of nature. I believe in God the Father, who also has a Son and a Spirit, mentioned later—a specific God, a Trinitarian God.

I believe in God the Father Almighty, who can do anything that he wants to do—whether I believe in him or not! He will accomplish everything he sets out to do. I depend on this God for my existence, my sustenance, and my salvation. Without him I wouldn't be here at all, and if I get to take another breath it is all because of him. I owe my place, in this creation and the next, to him alone.

Belief and balance

This belief I am declaring is relational, not merely informational. It's not just about what I believe in my head but what I balance my life on.

So it is an intellectual faith that I am confessing in the Creed. I start by saying that all my thoughts begin with an Almighty Father God, and about how everything somehow relates to him. My *credo* is not something I strap on every Sunday but can easily jettison when I work, rest, or play. It's something that goes with me everywhere and informs all I do and say and long for. But it is also a personal faith. Being a Christian is not ultimately an ideology or a philosophy, but a relationship to a Father, from whom I draw comfort, strength, acceptance, love, identity, security, and hope. He is a Father I can believe in, and entrust myself to with confidence. People may disappoint, but because he is almighty, God will never let me down.

A privileged relationship

God the Father is first and foremost a Father in his relationship to God the Son. He is not "male" as opposed to female. For a start, he is "without body" as Article 1 of the Church of England's *Thirty-nine Articles* puts it, a spirit without sex as we physical mortals understand it. However, Christians have always spoken of God as "the Father", because this is his relation to the Son within the godhead, and the name he himself chooses, revealed to us in Scripture. It is not about his relationship to us, primarily, but his eternal relationship to another person in the Trinity.

God is our Lord, creator, judge, refuge. And he becomes our Father, when we are born again by his grace and he gives us the special privilege of becoming children of God (John 1:12). He is first and foremost the Father of our Lord Jesus Christ (1 Peter 1:3). But Jesus himself teaches us to pray to God as "*Our* Father..." He is not our Uncle, our Mother, or our Pet. He wants to be known as Father.

So in the Creed we take that intimate name upon our lips and dare to say we believe and trust in him. "See what great love the Father has lavished on us," the Apostle John rejoiced, "that we should be called children of God! And that is what we are!" (1 John 3:1). It is an immense privilege to call him Father.

Questions for Reflection

1. What does it mean for us that God is *our* Father, as well as the eternal Father?

2. What difference does it make to know that God is Almighty?

3. Why do some people find it difficult to acknowledge their dependence on God?

Prayer

Almighty God, our heavenly Father,
you are unchanging and all powerful:
renew us by your Spirit and inspire us with your love,
that we may know you, the only true God,
and Jesus Christ whom you have sent,
and in whose name we pray,
Amen.

The Most Profound Truths

Creator of Heaven and Earth

*"The earth is the Lord's, and everything in it, the world,
and all who live in it; for he founded it on the seas and
established it on the waters."*

Psalm 24:1-2

The short phrase "creator of heaven and earth" takes no
more than 3 seconds to say, but it contains the most profound truths about God, the universe, and us.

The creator God

The God we believe in, the Father Almighty, is a creative being. Behind the beauty and order of the universe is a creator, not random chance. A careful and deliberate personal creator is responsible for everything, not impersonal and blind "forces of nature."

This means that God is above and beyond the world. He is not our creation, but we are his. He is not the product of primitive human fantasies, as some claim. We are the fruit of *his* imagination.

There was a time when we did not exist, when nothing existed—except God. Then, there was a moment of genesis. "In the beginning God created the heavens and the earth" (Genesis 1:1).

The ordered universe

"There are more things in heaven and earth", Shakespeare's Hamlet tells his friend Horatio, "than are dreamt of in your philosophy" (Hamlet, Act 1, scene 5). Horatio was having a hard time swallowing something his rational mind could not understand and his hands could not touch. The Creed also reminds us that there is more to the universe than just earth and whatever physics, maths, chemistry, and biology can describe. Our God is the creator of the heavens, as well as of the earth.

The word "heavens" refers in the Bible to the sky above where birds and aeroplanes fly, and to the great expanse where the sun, moon, and stars twinkle away to give us light and an indication of time and seasons (Genesis 1:14-15). Yet it can also refer to the place from which God speaks and acts, his dwelling place (1 Kings 8:30). It is the place where angels come from (Matthew 18:10). The Lord our God is the maker "of all things visible and invisible" (as the Nicene Creed puts it).

He made mountains, trees, seas, lakes, streams, animals, vegetables, and minerals. DNA, gravity, magnetism, and love were all his idea, along with colour, taste, texture, hot, cold, wet, and dry. It would take pages and pages to describe the huge variety of things with which our creator God has blessed the world. There are around 30,000 species of fish, and more than 60,000 types of tree in the world. Amazingly, there are over 300,000 varieties of beetle. All designed and intricately put together by a divine master craftsman. Yet we don't know the half of it—how much is yet to be discovered in unseen realms of creation we could barely conceive of?

None of this is an accident. It is purposeful and intentional. When I look around, I see his handiwork everywhere. It is marred and broken in many ways, because sin has entered the world. But sparks of beauty and strength remain, and God's fingerprints are everywhere. He made space, time, and matter—and since he made it, we know matter matters; God is not just interested in "spiritual" things, but in flesh and blood and bodies too.

We are his creatures

The fact that our God is the maker of heaven and earth leaves no space for any other God. He has no rival. There are no other gods with their own independent empires. It's true that we humans are made in his image, but there is a very firm distinction between creatures and their creator. We are made in his image, not he in ours, and we belong—body and soul—to him.

As Psalm 24 says, everything and everyone belongs to God, for (because) he made them. Creation gives him a right of ownership over us. Our role is to be stewards of the gifts he has generously given us. The earth does not belong to us. So we must ultimately answer to him for how we treat his creation: how we look after it, what we do to develop it, and not least how we treat others in it who are made in his image.

Questions for Reflection

1. Which aspects of God's handiwork in creation fill you most with awe and joy?

2. What difference does it make to believe in a personal, creator God rather than blind chance?

3. Why is it important to remember the distinction between us as creatures and God as creator?

Prayer

Lord our God, creator and possessor of heaven and earth,
commander of angels, and master of time and space:
give us eyes to see the wonder and design of your ordered creation,
that we may rejoice in your goodness
and steward the earth with gladness
as those who bear your image.
In Jesus's name we pray,
Amen.

The Author of Perfect Happiness

I believe in Jesus Christ

"Jesus performed many other signs in the presence of his disciples, which are not recorded in this book. But these are written that you may believe that Jesus is the Messiah, the Son of God, and that by believing you may have life in his name."

John 20:30-31

To say, "I believe" is a radical thing to do in our world. And that is especially so when the things we believe in cannot be seen. To say "I believe in Jesus Christ" means several things here in the Creed. For a start, it means we believe he exists, even though we can't now see him. It also means we believe what he says, in a world that is not certain what is true and what is fake news. And finally, it means we entrust ourselves to Jesus Christ, as well as to God the Father Almighty.

The existence of Jesus

To believe in Jesus means at the very least that we believe in his existence. When we talk about Jesus, it is not make-believe, a game. He is not a fictional character. Fictional characters can be inspiring—like Princess Leia or Spiderman or Wonder Woman or Frodo

Baggins. I confess to being inspired by Vice Admiral Holdo from the film, *The Last Jedi*. She's awesome. But sane and sensible people don't "believe in" those people, the way Christians believe in Jesus Christ.

To say we believe in Jesus is saying that we believe in a specific, real person who actually existed (in fact, he actually still exists, and is alive—but let's not get ahead of ourselves!). Jesus was born a Jewish man, living in Israel at a time of Roman occupation over 2000 years ago. The Gospels—that is, the biographies of him in the Bible—give us detailed genealogies so we can locate him in time and space as part of a particular nation, a particular tribe, a particular family.

Those Gospels also give us his context and backstory, and an amazing amount of detail about his life and work. As Peter, one of his closest companions, once said, "God anointed Jesus of Nazareth with the Holy Spirit and power, and he went around doing good and healing all who were under the power of the devil, because God was with him. We are witnesses of everything he did in the country of the Jews and in Jerusalem." (Acts 10:38-39).

Because of these things that he did, and especially because of his death and resurrection, his early followers came to believe that Jesus is the Christ, or Messiah. What does that mean? Christ is a title (not a surname) and it means "anointed one", a special, chosen king. It means, as the theologian John Calvin once put it, that "he had been promised in the Old Testament Law and the Prophets, as the Mediator between God and people, the Father's highest Ambassador, the only Restorer of the world, and the Author of perfect happiness."

Listening to Jesus

There is more to it than simply believing that Jesus exists. No serious historian ever doubted his existence! When we say "I believe you", we tend to assume the other person's existence. What we mean by it is that we believe what the other person is saying. It is the same with Jesus. To say that we believe in Jesus Christ means that we give him credence. We give him credit. It means we listen to him.

You may believe in a cause, a particular politician or party, or in the truthfulness of the BBC or a specific newspaper—though in our cynical age it is not always easy to trust in such things. To believe means that we think they are credible and convincing. But to say "I believe in Jesus Christ" means that above all the other voices which call out for my attention and approval and action today, I give priority to his. We consider his claims and his teaching to be true and worthy of our acceptance.

Trusting in Jesus

To say "I believe in Jesus Christ" puts Jesus on the same level in the Creed as the Father and the Holy Spirit. "I believe in God, the Father Almighty… and in Jesus Christ… and I believe in the Holy Spirit." This is staggering, and we will think more about it later on in this book.

But to say we believe in him means more than that we believe he exists or that we will listen to him. We don't simply click "Follow", to be entertained or amused or occasionally inspired by him as we might be by others, on social media perhaps. We are declaring our eternal confidence in Jesus. We rest our very lives on him, so that we no longer trust in our wealth or our looks or our ability to see us through this life.

This is not just an academic opinion—it is a profound life choice, with drastic implications now and forever. Because as the apostle John (another of Jesus's closest friends) says, the Gospels were written "that you may believe that Jesus is the Messiah, the Son of God, and that by believing you may have life in his name."

Questions for Reflection

1. Why are many people today resistant to actually reading the Gospels about Jesus, which are far shorter than most modern novels?

2. Which voices (apart from Jesus's) do your friends tend to listen to and respect the most, and what impact does that have on their lives?

3. Jesus is the Christ, "the Author of perfect happiness", but what else do your friends look to, to make them perfectly happy?

Prayer

Lord Jesus Christ,
who came to this earth that we may have life
and have it in abundance:
grant us grace to believe and trust in you
so that by believing in your words of promise and truth
we may have everlasting life,
Amen.

Who's the boss of you?

I believe in… God's Only Son, our Lord

"After six days Jesus took with him Peter, James and John the brother of James, and led them up a high mountain by themselves. There he was transfigured before them. His face shone like the sun, and his clothes became as white as the light. Just then there appeared before them Moses and Elijah, talking with Jesus. Peter said to Jesus, 'Lord, it is good for us to be here. If you wish, I will put up three shelters—one for you, one for Moses and one for Elijah.' While he was still speaking, a bright cloud covered them, and a voice from the cloud said, 'This is my Son, whom I love; with him I am well pleased. Listen to him!'"
Matthew 17:1-5

All of us are defined in some way by our relationships. I am who I am in relationship to others: the son of Gordon and Denise; the husband of Kerry; the father of Joshua, Cara, and Lucy; the Director of Church Society, and the boss of David, Ros, Mark, George, and Sophie. The next line in the Apostles' Creed tells us two things about Jesus's relationships: he is the only Son of God the Father, and he's our Lord.

The Son of God

Mark 1:1 announces that it is "The beginning of the good news of Jesus the Messiah, the Son of God." Jesus's cousin, John the Baptist, called Jesus "the Son of God" or "God's Chosen One"

(John 1:34), as did his disciples (Matthew 14:33; John 1:49; John 11:27). But Mark also tells us that "Whenever the impure spirits saw him, they fell down before him and cried out, 'You are the Son of God'" (Mark 3:11), and even the Roman centurion who looked on as Jesus died declared, "Surely this man was the Son of God!" (Mark 15:39) They knew he was different to ordinary men.

Jesus himself always claimed to have a very close and unique relationship with God his Father. "Anyone who has seen me has seen the Father," he said, and "I am in the Father and the Father is in me" (see John 14:8-11). Which is why it is so important to believe in both the Father and the Son, because "No one who denies the Son has the Father; whoever acknowledges the Son has the Father also" (1 John 2:23). Jesus even said that just believing in "God" was not enough, because "Whoever does not honour the Son does not honour the Father, who sent him" (John 5:23).

We may be children of God, as believers. But that is by the grace of adoption, through faith alone. Jesus is the Son of God by nature. It is in that sense that he is "God's *only* Son"—or as the Nicene Creed puts it, "the only begotten Son of God, begotten of the Father before all ages, God from God, Light from Light, true God from true God, begotten, not made, of one being with the Father." This is why in the passage at the top of this chapter, the Father calls Jesus "my Son, whom I love; with him I am well pleased."

Our Lord

Being the Son of God is something Jesus is by nature. But the other title mentioned here in the Creed is something he *becomes*: our Lord. The word "Lord" means Master. That is what Jesus is to us, his people. In a sense he is the Lord of all creation, the ruler and boss of everything and everyone. But in a more intimate and special sense, he is the Master of those who follow him and listen to him. He is not just *the* Lord, but *our* Lord, when we submit to him and obey his command to repent of our sins and believe in him.

As I mentioned above, even demons recognised Jesus for who he is, the only Son of God. But it is not enough to make a difference in our lives, if all we do is acknowledge him for who he is. We need willingly to bow down to him as Lord, and gladly accept his rule over our lives. That's what it means to be a Christian—to give up the reins, hand over the wheel, and let Jesus be in charge and make the rules rather than us.

One day, "at the name of Jesus every knee will bow, in heaven and on earth and under the earth, and every tongue confess that Jesus Christ is Lord, to the glory of God the Father" (Philippians 2:10-11). Some will submit of their own accord with joy, but others will only reluctantly kneel in obedience. The big question for all of us is this: will we let Jesus be our Lord now, so he can also be our saviour—or will we stubbornly try to resist him, and only meet him as our judge?

Questions for Reflection

1. Have you consciously and deliberately submitted to Jesus as your Lord?

2. What difference does it make in your life to recognise Jesus as your Master?

3. Why is it reassuring that if you're a Christian, your master is also the unique Son of God?

Prayer

Gracious heavenly Father,
who sent your only Son into the world
to save all those who believe and trust in him as Lord:
give us grace to honour his name and listen to his word
that with the daily help of your Holy Spirit
we may live as his true disciples,
Amen.

The Miracle of Christmas

Jesus Christ… was conceived by the Holy Spirit and born of the Virgin Mary

"'How will this be,' Mary asked the angel, 'since I am a virgin?' The angel answered, 'The Holy Spirit will come on you, and the power of the Most High will overshadow you. So the holy one to be born will be called the Son of God. Even Elizabeth your relative is going to have a child in her old age, and she who was said to be unable to conceive is in her sixth month. For no word from God will ever fail.' 'I am the Lord's servant,' Mary answered. 'May your word to me be fulfilled.' Then the angel left her."

Luke 1:34-38

This part of the Apostles' Creed is about the greatest of all God's miracles: the miracle of Christmas. It tells us about the two natures of Christ. It is essential to Christianity that the Lord Jesus is not only human, but also divine. He is a God-man.

The process by which this happened is called the incarnation. God took on human flesh in the womb of the Virgin Mary, and was born nine months later on that first Christmas day. The Athanasian Creed (a longer creed, all about the Trinity and the incarnation) puts it this way: "Now, the right faith is that we should believe and confess that our Lord Jesus Christ, the Son of God, is both God and man equally. He is God from the Being of the Father, begotten before the worlds, and he is man from the being of his mother, born in the world; perfect God and perfect man."

The Apostles' Creed tells us about Jesus's two natures by telling us about where he got them from. So let's examine what it says under two headings.

The Holy Spirit

So, first, Jesus did not have a human father. He was conceived by the Holy Spirit, not by Joseph. It was God who took the initiative in the incarnation, just as he is always the one who makes the first move in our salvation.

Joseph himself knew this. An angel appeared to him in a dream saying, "Joseph son of David, do not be afraid to take Mary home as your wife, because what is conceived in her is from the Holy Spirit" (Matthew 1:20). The child was to be given two names: Jesus, which means "the Lord saves"; and Immanuel, which means "God with us."

So Jesus was more than a man. Although this makes complete sense of the rest of his life (his character and his work) and the fact that millions throughout the world and across history have given their lives to him, it is hard for many people to accept, because it is a miracle. It seems much easier to assume that Mary was lying about her virginity and that she and Joseph tried to cover up their lapse in sexual purity by blaming the baby on God! But that would unravel the whole truthfulness of the Bible and its prophecies. It would put all other miracles in doubt as well—including Jesus's resurrection, on which our entire hope depends, but which seems equally difficult to believe if one cannot think outside the limitations of this world.

The Virgin Mary

Jesus was, however, also truly a man. He was not a divine ghost who just appeared to be human. He took real human nature from his mother, Mary, who willingly gave her body so that he might be born into the world from her. As the Church of England's *Thirty-nine Articles* put it, the Son of God "took Man's nature in the womb of the blessed Virgin, of her substance: so that two whole and perfect Natures, that is to say, the Godhead and Manhood, were joined together in one Person, never to be divided" (Article 2).

The fact that Immanuel, God with us, would be born from a virgin mother was prophesied in the Bible around 700 years before it happened. Isaiah 7:14 says "Therefore the Lord himself will give you a sign: The virgin will conceive and give birth to a son, and will call him Immanuel." When Mary heard it was going to be her, she was startled but replied, "I am the Lord's servant. May your word to me be fulfilled" (Luke 1:38). She believed, as the angel said, that nothing is impossible with God. So she is a wonderful example of submissive, obedient trust in God's promises, even when those promises seem humanly unbelievable.

Jesus was conceived by the Holy Spirit and born of a virgin. He did not inherit that selfish twist of nature which curls us in on ourselves. That's why the Bible emphasises his sinlessness (see Hebrews 4:15 or 2 Corinthians 5:21), which is an astonishing claim from his own lips (John 8:29, 46) but even more so from the pen of his intimate friend, Peter, who knew him better than most (1 Peter 2:22-24). By contrast, his brothers and sisters (mentioned in Mark 3:31 and 6:3-4) were not sinless.

Mary is very different to some of the other women named in Jesus's family tree in Matthew 1:1-17. They are adulterers and prostitutes, but she is a faithful virgin. Yet this does not mean that Mary herself was sinless: she needed saving as much as every son of Adam and daughter of Eve, which is why she says "My soul glorifies the Lord and my spirit rejoices in God *my Saviour*" (Luke 1:47). Jesus's perfect human nature comes from a long line of people who proved to be fragile, fallen, and fallible; but this is precisely why he is given the name Jesus, "because he will save *his people* from their sins" (Matthew 1:21). Despite our sin, we too can be his people, if we trust in God's gracious word as Mary did.

Questions for Reflection

1. What parts of Jesus's life only really make sense if he is more than a mere man?

2. How does Mary's faith inspire you to act on the promises of God which you find most difficult to believe?

3. Why should it be an encouragement to us that Jesus was born into a sinful family tree as part of a sinful nation who were at the time experiencing oppression and difficulty?

Prayer

Almighty God,
who gave us your only Son
to take our nature upon him and to be born of a faithful virgin:
grant that we, who are born again in him
and made your children by adoption and grace,
may daily be renewed by your Holy Spirit
and learn to trust every one of your promises.
In Jesus's name we pray,
Amen.

The Crucial Moment

**He suffered under Pontius Pilate,
was crucified, died, and was buried.**

He descended to the dead.

"*Then Pilate took Jesus and had him flogged… Finally Pilate
handed him over to them to be crucified. So the soldiers took charge
of Jesus. Carrying his own cross, he went out to the place of the Skull
(which in Aramaic is called Golgotha). There they crucified him, and
with him two others—one on each side and Jesus in the middle…*

*Later, knowing that everything had now been finished, and so that
Scripture would be fulfilled, Jesus said, 'I am thirsty'. A jar of wine
vinegar was there, so they soaked a sponge in it, put the sponge on
a stalk of the hyssop plant, and lifted it to Jesus's lips. When he had
received the drink, Jesus said, 'It is finished'. With that, he bowed his
head and gave up his spirit…*

*The soldiers therefore came and broke the legs of the first man who
had been crucified with Jesus, and then those of the other. But when
they came to Jesus and found that he was already dead, they did not
break his legs. Instead, one of the soldiers pierced Jesus's side with a
spear, bringing a sudden flow of blood and water… Taking Jesus's
body, the two of them wrapped it, with the spices, in strips of linen.
This was in accordance with Jewish burial customs. At the place
where Jesus was crucified, there was a garden, and in the garden a
new tomb, in which no one had ever been laid. Because it was the
Jewish day of Preparation and since the tomb was nearby, they laid
Jesus there.*" John 19:1-42

So far the Apostles' Creed has been mind-blowing in its claims about God's power and authority. He is the Father Almighty, the creator of everything. And we have heard about Jesus, the Son of this Almighty God, and our Lord and Master, who took human flesh in a breathtaking miracle of divine humility. But today we are looking at the most awe-inspiring teaching of Christianity—that when God became man, he did it in order to suffer and die for us.

Suffering

The Creed says Jesus suffered, in a particular time and place, "under Pontius Pilate." Pilate was the Prefect of the province of Judea from AD 26 to 36, under the Roman Emperor Tiberius. Jesus's public ministry took place during his time in charge of the area, centred on Jerusalem. This all happened to a real person at a specific moment in history.

We are not simply thinking of the execution of Jesus here, but of all his suffering during that time. That could refer to his whole life: suffering all the stresses and indignities of physical human existence; the opposition of sinful men and women who hated him and plotted against him throughout his ministry, despite his great miracles of power and kindness; his temptation and his trial; and the flogging Jesus received from Pilate, even when he had been found innocent of all charges. As the apostle Peter says, to all those who suffer in this life, "Christ suffered for you, leaving you an example, that you should follow in his steps" (1 Peter 2:21). He suffered without ever sinning.

Crucifixion

It is noteworthy that the Creed has very little on Jesus's life. It goes straight from his birth almost immediately to his death. In the Gospels, there is also a huge amount of space given to the final week of his life. This is the crucial moment for world history, and for our faith: the immortal Son of God, died. There's a reason that the cross is the sign of our faith.

Crucifixion was a painfully brutal way to die, though the Bible doesn't dwell on the gory details so much as on the plain fact. The Romans used this form of execution many times. A crucified messiah wasn't a very popular idea in a context where crucifixion was reserved for the lowest of the low. "The utterly vile death of the cross" as some called it, wasn't spoken of at all in polite society without a twinge of disgust. Crucifixion was reserved for barbarians, slaves, and peasants—the scum of the earth. So to worship a crucified God was simply madness in this context— this is why ancient writers called Christianity a "sick delusion" and "a senseless and crazy superstition." Why would anyone want to worship a *crucified* God?

It is also particularly significant biblically that Jesus was crucified. Because in the Old Testament it says that anyone executed and hung on a tree like this was cursed by God (Deuteronomy 21:23). "They pierce my hands and my feet" says the man under attack who feels forsaken by God (Psalm 22:16). In the New Testament, the apostle Paul says that because of this, "Christ redeemed us from the curse of the law by becoming a curse for us" (Galatians 3:13). What he did, he did "for us and for our salvation" as the Nicene Creed puts it—he didn't have to die at all, but "he was pierced for our transgressions" (Isaiah 53:5), to absorb the curse of God that we deserve, in our place, so we don't have to.

Death

The Creed is explicit that Jesus wasn't just crucified. Sometimes, it was just possible to survive a few hours of crucifixion and to live on for a while—though it would take some time to recover (and you wouldn't look or feel great afterwards). But Jesus died. Some have suggested that he may have just fainted, and people thought he was dead. But that is hard to square with the eyewitness testimony that his death was confirmed by hardened Roman soldiers who knew death when they saw it and pierced Jesus's side with a spear just to make sure. That little detail in John's Gospel, that blood and water came out when they did this, confirms that he was gone, because this is what happens when a body expires. Besides, if he had only swooned, he was hardly in a state to convince people a few days later that he was not just still clinging onto life but was in fact the risen Lord of glory!

Jesus was then buried in the usual way for Jewish people at that time. He descended to the place of the dead. He tasted death in all its physical and spiritual horror, and drank it to the dregs. There is no aspect of that terrible final curtain that he did not experience. So we know that when we face it one day ourselves, Jesus has emptied it of its ultimate power. As he himself now says, "I hold the keys of death and Hades" (Revelation 1:18).

Questions for Reflection

1. How can Jesus's sinless suffering be an example to us in our suffering?

2. How did God turn something so evil—the murder of his Son—into something so good?

3. Why is it important to stress that Jesus really died, was buried, and descended to the dead?

Prayer

Almighty God,
look with mercy upon your people,
for whom our Lord Jesus suffered death upon the cross:
grant us strength to take our cross up daily
and put to death our sinful desires,
that being united with him in his death,
we may rise with him in glory,
through Jesus Christ our Saviour,
Amen.

A New World

On the third day he rose again

"For what I received I passed on to you as of first importance: that Christ died for our sins according to the Scriptures, that he was buried, that he was raised on the third day according to the Scriptures, and that he appeared to Cephas, and then to the Twelve. After that, he appeared to more than five hundred of the brothers and sisters at the same time, most of whom are still living, though some have fallen asleep. Then he appeared to James, then to all the apostles, and last of all he appeared to me also, as to one abnormally born."

1 Corinthians 15:3-8

Having heard about the death of Jesus in the previous lines of the Creed, we now turn to the astonishing miracle of the resurrection. On the third day, Jesus rose again. We'll look at how this was predicted by Jesus and others: how it was emphatically *physical*; how it was a public event; in what ways it demonstrated Jesus's power; and how it was a pledge of our own resurrection.

Predicted

Jesus confidently predicted not only his death but also his resurrection, several times in the Gospels (e.g. Mark 8:31, 9:31, and 10:34). After it happened, Jesus said to his disciples:

"'This is what I told you while I was still with you: Everything must be fulfilled that is written about me in the Law of Moses, the Prophets and the Psalms.' Then he opened their minds so they could understand the Scriptures. He told them, 'This is what is written: The Messiah will suffer and rise from the dead on the third day'" (Luke 24:44-46).

The resurrection of the Messiah was prophesied in the Old Testament. Isaiah 53 contains a prophecy of the sacrificial death of God's Suffering Servant, and it also contains a hint that he will not remain dead: "though the LORD makes his life an offering for sin, he will see his offspring and prolong his days, and the will of the LORD will prosper in his hand. After he has suffered, he will see the light of life and be satisfied" (Isaiah 53:10-11).

The apostles also came to see in Psalm 16:9-10 a hint of what was to come: "Therefore my heart is glad and my tongue rejoices; my body also will rest secure, because you will not abandon me to the realm of the dead, nor will you let your faithful one see decay." The writer, who is asking God to preserve his life, is confident that his flesh will remain secure, because even if he ends up in Sheol (the place of the dead), God will not allow him to remain there and decay. This is why Paul writes in 1 Corinthians 15:4 that Christ was raised again on the third day "according to" or "in accordance with the Scriptures" (see also Acts 26:22-23). It should not have been a surprise!

Physical

Jesus's resurrection from the dead was not a party trick. He really did die. And when he rose again from the dead, he was not a ghost. He ate and drank with his disciples (Luke 24:41-43), which would be a bit icky if he was a ghost! Doubting Thomas was invited to touch the wounds Jesus still had from his death on the cross (John 20:24-28), and so were the others: "Look at my hands and my feet. It is I myself!" said Jesus. "Touch me and see; a ghost does not have flesh and bones, as you see I have" (Luke 24:39).

Public

Jesus appeared in public to his disciples. Paul lists some of the people he appeared to in the reading above from 1 Corinthians 15. He appeared to Cephas (another name for Simon Peter), to the twelve apostles, to Paul himself, and even to 500 people all at the same time. This couldn't possibly just be an hallucination or wishful thinking from deluded minds. Paul even says many of these witnesses were still alive as he was writing, so they could be interrogated and asked about it, and their reliability as witnesses assessed.

The truth was out there—and he had been seen and touched and heard by hundreds of people. If that was not true, the early Christian movement would have died out pretty quickly, like every other Messianic movement of that century. The logic of history suggests that the best explanation for why billions of people have since believed in the resurrection, is that it is—amazingly—true.

Powerful

Jesus said, before his death, that "The reason my Father loves me is that I lay down my life—only to take it up again. No one takes it from me, but I lay it down of my own accord. I have authority to lay it down *and authority to take it up again*. This command I received from my Father" (John 10:17-18). He did not have to die, but he expressed his power not by calling for twelve legions of angels to come and rescue him and show the Romans who was boss—but by voluntarily giving up his life.

He could do this because he had a cast iron promise from his Father that he also had authority and power to take up his life again afterwards. This is what they together decided even before he took flesh and was born. The resurrection proves that Jesus really was who he said he was all along: God's powerful Son. As Paul says: "through the Spirit of holiness he was appointed the Son of God in power by his resurrection from the dead" (Romans 1:4).

Pledge

Finally, the resurrection is a pledge to us of our own resurrection from the dead one day. By Jesus's power we too are raised up to a new life when we believe and trust in him. Our faith unites us to him, joins us to him in an inseparable bond, so his resurrection assures us that death is not the end for us either. The gates of death cannot defeat Jesus or his people.

Jesus is called "the firstborn from among the dead" (Colossians 1:18) and "the firstborn among many brothers and sisters" (Romans 8:29). When he rose again he wasn't just resuscitated, to die again another day (Romans 6:9). He entered and began a whole new world. That's why it happened "on the third day"—Friday, Saturday, *Sunday*. The Sabbath (Saturday) was the seventh day, so Sunday is the first day of the new week—and a new world.

Questions for Reflection

1. Why is it important to affirm that Jesus truly rose again *bodily*?

2. What does Jesus's resurrection tell us about our own future beyond death?

3. What are we saying by meeting together on Sunday (*the Lord's Day*, Revelation 1:10)?

Prayer

Almighty God,
through your Son, Jesus Christ, you have conquered death
and opened to us the gate of everlasting life:
captivate our minds with the glories of the world to come,
that our hearts may turn away
from the fading pleasures of this world
and be fixed on the risen Christ,
in whose powerful name we pray,
Amen.

Is Jesus a Spaceman?

He ascended into heaven

"When he had led them out to the vicinity of Bethany, he lifted up his hands and blessed them. While he was blessing them, he left them and was taken up into heaven. Then they worshipped him and returned to Jerusalem with great joy. And they stayed continually at the temple, praising God."

Luke 24:50-53

Where is Jesus now?

Jesus is not still here with us on earth, to prove his resurrection, or to continue teaching us himself. After his resurrection he eventually ascended into heaven.

This appears to be a little "science fiction" to some. And it seems difficult to believe in the age of space travel! But the point was not to show us the literal location of heaven, beyond the atmosphere. So what was it all about? Well, he ascended U.P. F.O.R. U.S.

Universal authority

The ascension demonstrates Christ's universal authority. The apostle Peter says that Jesus, "has gone into heaven and is at God's right hand—with angels, authorities and powers in submission to him" (1 Peter 3:22). So Jesus has ascended back to his Father's right hand, a position of power and majesty. As Paul also writes, God "seated him at his right hand in the heavenly realms, far above all rule and authority, power and dominion, and every name that is invoked, not only in the present age but also in the one to come. And God placed all things under his feet and appointed him to be head over everything for the church, which is his body, the fullness of him who fills everything in every way" (Ephesians 1:20-23).

Jesus "humbled himself by becoming obedient to death—even death on a cross!" He did that for us. But because of this, "*Therefore* God exalted him to the highest place and gave him the name that is above every name" (Philippians 2:8-9)—which is also for the benefit of his people, his church. Our Lord Jesus is exalted to the highest place of power and authority in the universe. From all eternity he enjoyed pre-eminence, but he gave it all up to become a man and to die on the cross. But now, in the ascension, he again takes up that supreme position.

Perfect salvation is accomplished

Having been sent by God the Father Almighty, he now returns from his mission to the right hand of God the Father Almighty (notice that this line in the Creed echoes the first).

The ascension marks the end of Jesus's physical earthly presence. His body is now located elsewhere. We are not told to expect any more surprise or secret appearances of the Lord. Except, that is, one final return, when he comes to judge the living and the dead. Until then, his work on earth is done. He has accomplished what he came to do—to live the perfect life that we could never live and die the death that we all deserve. Our salvation is assured—Jesus has done everything necessary to save us. The way between humanity and God is open again.

Or as Hebrews puts it, "he is able to save completely those who come to God through him." Why? Because "he always lives to intercede for them. Such a high priest truly meets our need—one who is holy, blameless, pure, set apart from sinners, exalted above the heavens" (Hebrews 7:25-26). Because he is exalted, he can save us completely.

Forgiveness is assured

The ascension isn't just something that happened to Jesus twenty centuries ago. It has very real and present implications for us. Because of the ascension, our forgiveness is assured. Hebrews 1:3 says, "After he had provided purification for sins, he sat down at the right hand of the Majesty in heaven." His work was done, so he sat down. And since the purification of our sins has been provided for and Jesus is on the throne, we're told in Hebrews 4:16 to "approach God's throne of grace with confidence, so that we may receive mercy and find grace to help us in our time of need."

Our own ascension

The ascension of Christ guarantees our own ascension to heaven. In Ephesians 1 we hear about how Jesus has been appointed as head over everything for the benefit of the church. But in chapter 2, Paul continues by saying that God "raised us up with Christ and *seated us with him* in the heavenly realms in Christ Jesus" (Ephesians 2:6). So if we are "in Christ" by believing in him, we have not only been raised to spiritual life with Jesus, we have also ascended with Jesus too.

Just as Jesus's resurrection from the dead assures us of our own resurrection from the dead, so his ascension also assures us of our ascension into heaven. It's so certain, Paul says we are already *seated* with Christ in the heavenly realms.

Ruling through his word

King Jesus rules his people from his throne in heaven. As Paul tells us, "When he ascended on high, he took many captives and gave gifts to his people." And what were those gifts? He gave "the apostles, the prophets, the evangelists, the pastors and teachers, to equip his people for works of service, so that the body of Christ may be built up" (Ephesians 4:11-12).

In other words, the ascended Christ gave us his word to rule us, and pastor-teachers to apply that word. So the sceptre by which our high king rules is his word, the Bible—the writings of the apostles and prophets faithfully proclaimed and applied to us by evangelists and pastors.

Unlimited Evangelism

As he ascended, Jesus said, "All authority in heaven and on earth has been given to me. Therefore go and make disciples of all nations, baptising them in the name of the Father and of the Son and of the Holy Spirit, and teaching them to obey everything I have commanded you" (Matthew 28:18-20). Acts also records Jesus saying to his disciples, "'you will receive power when the Holy Spirit comes on you; and you will be my witnesses in Jerusalem, and in all Judea and Samaria, and to the ends of the earth.' After he said this, he was taken up before their very eyes, and a cloud hid him from their sight" (Acts 1:8-9).

In other words, because of the ascension we must spread the gospel throughout the whole world. The ascended Jesus has all authority in heaven and on earth, and we are to declare that authority by preaching the gospel and making people into disciples of Christ. Not just a few people, but all nations. His authority is universal so our evangelism is unlimited.

Spirit sent by Jesus

Finally, the ascension is for our benefit because it enables the coming of the Holy Spirit. This is what Jesus said in John 16:7: "very truly I tell you, it is for your good that I am going away. Unless I go away, the Advocate will not come to you; but if I go, I will send him to you."

So Jesus leaves the earth and ascends into heaven, there to be seated at the right hand of God the Father. And once he is there, the Father gives him the authority to send the Holy Spirit. When he, the Helper, comes, he comes to fill us and to empower us, to fix our eyes on Jesus the founder and perfecter of our faith. "For the joy set before him he endured the cross, scorning its shame, and sat down at the right hand of the throne of God" (Hebrews 12:2).

Questions for Reflection

1. Why is it significant that Jesus is *seated* in heaven?

2. What is Jesus doing now?

3. What would you say to someone who said they had seen Jesus on earth?

Prayer

Almighty God,
whose Son Jesus Christ is now seated with you,
far above all rule and authority and power and dominion:
grant that in our hearts and minds we may also ascend there
and dwell continually with our perfect saviour,
who has sent his Holy Spirit
to empower us to spread your word throughout the world.
In his exalted name we pray,
Amen.

Nothing to Scoff at

He will come again to judge the living and the dead

"For you know very well that the day of the Lord will come like a thief in the night. While people are saying, 'Peace and safety,' destruction will come on them suddenly, as labour pains on a pregnant woman, and they will not escape. But you, brothers and sisters, are not in darkness so that this day should surprise you like a thief. You are all children of the light and children of the day. We do not belong to the night or to the darkness. So then, let us not be like others, who are asleep, but let us be awake and sober. For those who sleep, sleep at night, and those who get drunk, get drunk at night. But since we belong to the day, let us be sober, putting on faith and love as a breastplate, and the hope of salvation as a helmet. For God did not appoint us to suffer wrath but to receive salvation through our Lord Jesus Christ. He died for us so that, whether we are awake or asleep, we may live together with him."

1 Thessalonians 5:2-10

He will come again…

The Old Testament speaks many times about "the day of the LORD"—a day when God would come and put everything right that has gone wrong in this fallen world of his. In the New Testament it becomes clear that this day will ultimately be the one on which Jesus returns from heaven. As the disciples were told when Jesus ascended: "This same Jesus, who has been taken from you into heaven, will come back in the same way you have seen him go into heaven" (Acts 1:11).

Right at the end of the Bible we hear "He who testifies to these things says, 'Yes, I am coming soon.' Amen. Come, Lord Jesus!" (Revelation 22:20). He will not remain apart from us forever. He will come again. When I say the Creed, I always stress the "will" in this line—I firmly believe and hope in this promise, and long for that day when he *will* come again.

There have always been some who doubt it. The apostle Peter warned that "in the last days scoffers will come, scoffing and following their own evil desires. They will say, 'Where is this "coming" he promised? Ever since our ancestors died, everything goes on as it has since the beginning of creation'" (2 Peter 3:3-4). They use the apparent delay in Jesus's return to pursue their own sinful desires, thinking that tomorrow will always be just like today and nothing will ever happen to force them to stop. But the day is coming, and it is nothing to scoff at.

What will it be like? Revelation 1:7 says "Look, he is coming with the clouds, and every eye will see him, even those who pierced him." So it will not be enigmatic or obscure or secret. He won't just be appearing to the chosen few. This will be a dramatic and public event—indeed, the most dramatic and most public event in the history of the world. When it's time for Jesus to return from the glory he now enjoys with his Father in heaven, every single one of us will know it.

Perhaps you know what it's like to look forward eagerly to a visit from a distant friend or relative whose company you know you will always enjoy? The future we look forward to as Christians is like that, multiplied a billion—the presence of a person we love and long to see, restored to us at last. Later in the Creed we confess our belief in the resurrection of our bodies and the life everlasting. These are astounding blessings. But the very best thing about our future is that Jesus will be there. *He* will come again.

...to judge the living and the dead

Why is Jesus coming back? The Creed tells us that he is coming again to judge the living and the dead. The day of the Lord is the day of judgment. It is a day of reckoning for every single one of us, whether we are alive on that day or already dead.

Jesus said "When the Son of Man comes in his glory, and all the angels with him, he will sit on his glorious throne. All the nations will be gathered before him, and he will separate the people one from another as a shepherd separates the sheep from the goats" (Matthew 25:31-32). There are two destinations for those two groups of people. Some "will go away to eternal punishment," he says, "but the righteous to eternal life" (Matthew 25:46). These ultimate destinies are both eternal, everlasting, and final.

Your destination on that day will depend on Jesus, the judge. Either he will give you what you deserve or he will give you what you don't deserve. We all deserve hell, the bad place, "for the wages of sin is death" (Romans 6:23a) and we are all sinners who have fallen short of what God intended us to be. We've all stepped over the line in thought and word and deed. But on the other hand, for all those who repent and believe the good news, there is something undeserved: "the gift of God is eternal life in Christ Jesus our Lord" (Romans 6:23b). After all, "God so loved the world that he gave his one and only Son, that whoever believes in him shall not perish but have eternal life" (John 3:16).

The future of those who believe in Jesus is secure, because it relies on that promise from God, who "did not appoint us to suffer wrath but to receive salvation through our Lord Jesus Christ" (1 Thessalonians 5:9-10). Yet at the same time, the day of judgment will also be a day for specific rewards. As Paul declares, "we must all appear before the judgment seat of Christ, so that each of us may receive what is due us for the things done while in the body, whether good or bad" (2 Corinthians 5:10). Just how much we enjoy our first taste of eternity may depend on how much we have enjoyed pleasing the Lord of eternity with our earthly lives. As English cricketer and nineteenth-century missionary, C. T. Studd once wrote, "Only one life, 'twill soon be past, Only what's done for Christ will last."

The fact that there is a judgment day coming means that ultimately we do not have to worry about our worldly reputations, our worldly comforts, or our worldly securities. We can entrust ourselves to the one who judges justly (1 Peter 2:23), knowing that he will set everything straight one day with utter fairness and absolute impartiality, whatever happens to us here. There will be no cause for complaints or grounds for appeal on that day.

Questions for Reflection

1. How does the way you spend your life and your money reflect your belief in Jesus's return?

2. How does this part of the Creed motivate us when it comes to telling others about Jesus?

3. What profound injustices or secret faithfulnesses are you most looking forward to seeing rewarded on that day?

Prayer

Almighty God,
whose Son Jesus Christ came to us once in great humility
to die on the cross for our sins,
and will come again in glorious majesty
to judge the living and the dead:
give us grace to cast away the works of darkness
and to put on the armour of light,
now in the time of this mortal life,
that on that great and final day we may rise to the life immortal
and enter the joy of his presence,
in whose name we pray,
Amen.

Helper of the Weak

I believe in the Holy Spirit

*"Jesus said, 'If you love me, keep my commands. And I will ask
the Father, and he will give you another advocate to help you and be
with you forever—the Spirit of truth. The world cannot accept him,
because it neither sees him nor knows him. But you know him, for he
lives with you and will be in you."*

John 14:15-17

So far in the Creed we have declared our faith in the Father
who creates, and the Son who rescues. But the Christian
faith is a Trinitarian faith: we believe in one God in three
persons. Our God is Father, Son, and Spirit and always has been.
So now we turn to the Holy Spirit and his work of renewing.

The Spirit has already been mentioned in the Creed, when we
affirmed that Christ was "conceived by the Holy Spirit." So it is
clear that he has been involved in the work of our salvation from
the start. His work is to make us new, with new relationships and
a new community (*the church, the communion of saints*). He gives
us a new start (*the forgiveness of sins*), new bodies (*the resurrection
of the body*), and a new world (*the life everlasting*). We will look at
these in the next two chapters.

The Nicene Creed says much more about the Spirit than the
Apostles' Creed. It says:

"I believe in the Holy Spirit,

the Lord, the giver of life,
who proceeds from the Father and the Son.
With the Father and the Son he is worshipped and glorified.
He spoke through the prophets."

We will look more closely at the Holy Spirit by considering briefly who he is and what he does.

Who is the Holy Spirit?

As the Nicene Creed says, and the Bible affirms, the Holy Spirit is the Lord (2 Corinthians 3:17). He is God. We worship him and believe in him as a fully divine person (*not* "a part of God" as some loosely say), just as we worship and trust in the Father and the Son. That's why he makes an appearance here in the Creed.

In the early days of the church, the divine personhood of the Spirit was recognised. Jesus told his disciples to baptise people "in the name of the Father and of the Son and of the Holy Spirit" (Matthew 28:19). Just as Paul finished one of his letters with "May the grace of the Lord Jesus Christ, and the love of God, and the fellowship of the Holy Spirit be with you all" (2 Corinthians 13:14). These familiar texts make no sense if the Spirit is not both personal and divine. The apostle Peter also draws that parallel when he says, "Ananias, how is it that Satan has so filled your heart that you have lied to the Holy Spirit… You have not lied just to human beings but to God" (Acts 5:3-4).

Jesus calls him the Helper or Comforter (John 14:16, 26). He comes as Jesus's own successor and substitute—and anything less personal or less divine than Jesus would simply not be up to that job! The Spirit can be grieved (Isaiah 63:10; Ephesians 4:30), which is not an emotion that an impersonal force can experience.

The story of Jesus's baptism is a good one to remember here (Luke 3:21-22). As Jesus, the Son, was baptised, the Father spoke from heaven. At the same time, the Spirit took the form of a dove and rested upon Jesus. All three were there together. It isn't that God wears different masks: first he appears as Father (in the Old Testament) then he appears as Son (in the New Testament) and now he appears as Spirit. No, he was always Father, Son, and Holy Spirit at the same time. That's why we hear of the Spirit in the Old Testament too (e.g. Genesis 1:2; Exodus 31:3; Numbers 11:29; Judges 3:10; 2 Chronicles 24:20; Isaiah 11:2; Isaiah 42:1; Ezekiel 36:27; Joel 2:28).

What does the Holy Spirit do?

The Spirit is God and so he is involved in all that God does. He is not an instrument or force that God uses (or which we can "use"!). The Spirit himself IS God!

Just as certain aspects of God's work are particularly spoken of as works of the Father (he is the one who sends), or the Son (he is the one who comes to die for us), so certain aspects of God's work are especially related to the Spirit.

For example, he speaks through the prophets (Nehemiah 9:30; Zechariah 7:12). That's why it is said that "All Scripture is God-breathed" (2 Timothy 3:16). He convicts people of their sin, showing them their ungodliness and their need for Jesus (John 16:8-11). And he is the one who converts us, giving us new spiritual life (John 3:3-8), which new birth can be described as being "baptised by the Spirit" (1 Corinthians 12:13), something every true Christian has experienced whether they realise it or not.

The Spirit particularly helps those who follow Jesus. He is our Helper, and lives within us (John 14:17; Romans 8:9). He helps us especially to pray: "the Spirit helps us in our weakness. We do not know what we ought to pray for, but the Spirit himself intercedes for us through wordless groans… the Spirit intercedes for God's people in accordance with the will of God" (Romans 8:26-27).

The Spirit also leads us as believers (Galatians 5:18). To be led by him does not mean mystical inspirations or ecstatic highs. It doesn't mean visions and miracles for all. He leads us by helping us put to death evil desires and deeds (Romans 8:13). That will mean, ultimately, that we bear "the fruit of the Spirit" in our lives, and will grow in "love, joy, peace, forbearance, kindness, goodness, faithfulness, gentleness and self-control" (Galatians 5:22). None of these is optional, and none can be produced in us by our own efforts alone.

There are also various gifts mentioned in the Bible, which the Spirit gives to us for the common good not just for our own enjoyment. No-one has all of them. But all are given to help the church live well for Jesus, so we are like different parts of a body working together. Various gifts are listed in e.g. Romans 12:6-8, 1 Corinthians 7:7, 12:8-10 and 28-30, Ephesians 4:11, 1 Peter 4:10-11 (and Exodus 31:3). These are not exhaustive lists, but indicate some of the gifts which are given to believers by the Spirit in whom we believe.

Questions for Reflection

1. What would you say if someone asked you who the Holy Spirit is?

2. Why do those led by the Spirit bear the fruit of the Spirit (Galatians 5:22)?

3. What spiritual gift or gifts do you have, and are you using it/ them for the wider good?

Prayer

Almighty God,
whose Holy Spirit enables us to discern your will
and desire your way:
cleanse the thoughts of our hearts by the power of your Spirit,
that we may perfectly love you and rejoice in your word,
using the gifts that you give us to build up your church.
In Jesus's name we pray,
Amen.

Mother Church

The holy catholic church

"For through him we both have access to the Father by one Spirit. Consequently, you are no longer foreigners and strangers, but fellow citizens with God's people and also members of his household, built on the foundation of the apostles and prophets, with Christ Jesus himself as the chief cornerstone. In him the whole building is joined together and rises to become a holy temple in the Lord. And in him you too are being built together to become a dwelling in which God lives by his Spirit."

Ephesians 2:18-22

Trusting in the Church?

It is important to point out that when we say we believe in the holy catholic church, we are not saying we believe in an institution in the same way that we trust in God the Father, God the Son, and God the Holy Spirit. We are not declaring our faith in the church to save us, or asserting that all the pronouncements of a particular denomination or local fellowship are infallible and perfect. We don't in that sense believe "in" the church.

Our minds rest on God as true, and our confidence is fully satisfied in him alone. The Holy Spirit has spoken to us in the pages of scripture and what he says is utterly sufficient for our life as Christians, so we don't need any further sources of divine revelation and guidance. What the Creed is alerting us to, however, is that Christ has created for himself *a people*, and didn't just save you or me as isolated individuals. It is not just about "me and Jesus", but about being part of Christ's body, the church.

Mother Church

As the theologian John Calvin put it, everyone who has God as their Father, must also have the church as their mother, since we grow up as Christians under the care and nurture of the church. We confess that we are "members of the household of God" before we get to those parts of the Creed that are about personal salvation, so to speak. It is through the ministry and fellowship of the church that we normally come to know and enjoy the salvation we have in Christ.

We believe we have fellowship in the body which Christ calls his own. By faith we are united in that happy company. There is only one such body, one holy catholic church, because you can't tear Christ into little pieces so that he has 2 or 3 or 100 bodies. The word "catholic" in the Creed here means universal, worldwide. It does not mean *Roman* Catholic, as if we were affirming that we are part of that particular denomination or that we give that any authority. Indeed, we are actually saying the opposite: that we believe in the universal church and not simply the Roman part of it!

As members of the community which Christ died to save and which the Spirit is creating to be set apart from the world, we have a new identity and a new loyalty. Whatever our ethnic background, our nationality, our language, our football team, our political party—however we chose to identify ourselves to others in the world before we were Christians—above *all* these things we are now a part of the universal church of Jesus Christ, and children of one heavenly Father.

Fellowship with the saints

Each local church is the visible outcrop of the one universal church. We are God's army, tasked with recapturing the world from evil by spreading the good news of Jesus and living it out together, to bring light into a dark world. To do this we must stick together, because we need each other. As Paul puts it, "speaking the truth in love, we will grow to become in every respect the mature body of him who is the head, that is, Christ. From him the whole body, joined and held together by every supporting ligament, grows and builds itself up in love, as each part does its work" (Ephesians 4:15-16). Christ is our Head, but we need the different parts of the body to hold us together and help us to grow.

This is the communion of the saints. Again here we have to be careful with how we define certain words. In some circles, to be a "saint" means to be especially holy and good, to be a super-Christian perhaps, with miraculous powers or exceptional devotion. Over the centuries certain Christians have acquired the title "Saint" (e.g. St Paul, St Augustine) as if it was reserved for a special elite believer. That is not the way this word is used in the Creed, or indeed in the Bible. There we find that "holy ones" or "saints" is a name given to all God's people.

Also, "communion" here does not refer to the Lord's Supper or Holy Communion, sharing the bread and wine as Jesus taught us. It means our fellowship, our partnership, our joining together with other Christians (which may of course include sharing bread and wine together, but also so much more than that).

The communion we have as God's saints is that we are part of something which unites heaven and earth, angels and humans— all those who are chosen by God whether they are alive on earth now or safely in heaven with Christ (see Hebrews 12:22-23 and Ephesians 1:10). That does not mean we can talk to angels or to the dead, or that they are watching our every move and can intervene to help us if we ask them. We pray to God alone. Rather, it means we are part of something so much bigger than ourselves, and that "in Christ" we have unity with all the saints, alive or dead. They are our family, but especially those who are here on earth with us, to whom we have an especial responsibility.

Questions for Reflection

1. What part did the church play in your coming to faith in Christ?

2. What part does the church play in helping you to stay a Christian and grow in Christ?

3. How does your membership of the universal church relate to your lesser loyalties and identities (e.g. your "tribal" group or sporting preference or personal characteristics)?

Prayer

Almighty God,
who has set apart all your chosen people in one universal church,
the body of your Son Jesus Christ our Lord:
grant us grace so to follow the godly examples of your people
and build one another up in love and good deeds,
that we may come to those unspeakable joys,
which you have prepared for all those who truly love you;
through Jesus Christ our Lord,
Amen.

The Blessings of the Gospel

I believe in the forgiveness of sins, the resurrection of the body, and the life everlasting

"While they were eating, Jesus took bread, and when he had given thanks, he broke it and gave it to his disciples, saying, 'Take and eat; this is my body.' Then he took a cup, and when he had given thanks, he gave it to them, saying, 'Drink from it, all of you. This is my blood of the covenant, which is poured out for many for the forgiveness of sins. I tell you, I will not drink from this fruit of the vine from now on until that day when I drink it new with you in my Father's kingdom.'"

Matthew 26:26-29

In the final line of the Creed, we see three of the great blessings of being a Christian which are ours by believing in the gospel: our sins are forgiven, our bodies will one day be raised from death, and we will live forever with Jesus. We will be physical, and forgiven, forever.

Sins forgiven

We all know that sinking feeling in the pit of our stomachs, which we get when we know we have done something we shouldn't have. Our consciences assault us with the pain of guilt, telling us that something is wrong. There's nothing we can do to erase that feeling or cover it up, unless we burn away the sensitive tenderness of it by burying it away deep down in our souls, or find forgiveness from the person we have offended against. Sometimes that is not possible, and we cannot shake the guilty ache until we are punished by due authority for what we have done.

"If you, LORD, kept a record of sins, Lord, who could stand? But with you there is forgiveness, so that we can, with reverence, serve you" (Psalm 130:3-4). If God wrote down everything we ever thought, or said, or did which displeased him, then used that as evidence against us on judgment day, we would have to face his righteous anger forever. The Bible says of Jesus that "The punishment that brought us peace was on him" (Isaiah 53:5), so if we are united to him we are declared "not guilty" and forgiven. Which is why Christians have a right to smile, because in his mercy, God has released us from the crushing weight of guilt, shame, and despair which we truly deserve, and given us freedom to start afresh with him each day. We rely on and rejoice in the forgiveness of sins which is ours when we repent and believe.

Resurrection bodies

Human beings consist of body and soul united. Our bodies originate in the dust of the earth and our souls or spirits were breathed into us by God (Genesis 2:7). When we die, because of sin, this creative process is dramatically reversed and undone: "the dust returns to the ground it came from, and the spirit returns to God who gave it" (Ecclesiastes 12:7). This is not the way God intended us to be. We were intended for something more permanent and glorious.

After death, believers go to be with Jesus, "which is better by far" (Philippians 1:23), and we revel in the joy of his presence. But we are not meant to exist forever without a body. One day,

"Multitudes who sleep in the dust of the earth will awake: some to everlasting life, others to shame and everlasting contempt" (Daniel 12:2). We will be raised and given new bodies, with which to enjoy the new creation. This will happen "in a moment, in the twinkling of an eye, at the last trumpet. For the trumpet will sound, and the dead will be raised imperishable, and we shall be changed" (1 Corinthians 15:52). We will no longer sin, or even want to sin. So death will be no more.

Everlasting life

Some people think that the idea of life which goes on forever will be boring. But the everlasting life that God has planned for those who believe and trust in him will be so utterly brilliant that we will never want it to end. Jesus will wipe away every tear from our eyes, as crying and dying are abolished forever (Revelation 21:4). Every pleasure and joy we have ever known will be intensified and multiplied and sanctified. This life will last forever, but its quality will be spectacularly enhanced too, in ways that we cannot now even imagine.

The Reformer Martin Luther once wrote that "Though I am a great doctor, I haven't yet progressed beyond the Ten Commandments, the Creed, and the Lord's Prayer. I still learn and pray these every day. Who understands in all of its implications even the opening words?" If we have found that to be true in our faltering attempts to get to grips with the Apostles' Creed over the last few chapters, how much more will we struggle to wrap our puny minds around the glories to be revealed when all our hopes and yearnings begin to take shape in a new world?

When we've been there 10,000 years
Bright shining as the sun
We've no less days
To sing God's praise
Than when we first begun."

John Newton, from "Amazing Grace."

Questions for Reflection

1. Why do we not give thanks to God more often for the forgiveness of our sins?

2. What are you most looking forward to about your new resurrection body?

3. What are you most looking forward to about eternal life with Jesus beyond death?

Prayer

Gracious heavenly Father,
who forgives all those who truly repent
and believe the gospel of your Son Jesus Christ:
by the power of your Spirit,
give us patient endurance through the trials of this life,
that we may embrace and forever hold fast
the joyful hope of everlasting life,
which you have given us in our Saviour Jesus Christ.
In his name we pray,
Amen.

The Ten Commandments

And God spoke all these words:

"I am the Lord your God, who brought you out of Egypt, out of the land of slavery.

You shall have no other gods before me.

You shall not make for yourself an image in the form of anything in heaven above or on the earth beneath or in the waters below. You shall not bow down to them or worship them; for I, the Lord your God, am a jealous God, punishing the children for the sin of the parents to the third and fourth generation of those who hate me, but showing love to a thousand generations of those who love me and keep my commandments.

You shall not misuse the name of the Lord your God, for the Lord will not hold anyone guiltless who misuses his name.

Remember the Sabbath day by keeping it holy. Six days you shall labor and do all your work, but the seventh day is a sabbath to the Lord your God. On it you shall not do any work, neither you, nor your son or daughter, nor your male or female servant, nor your animals, nor any foreigner residing in your towns. For in six days the Lord made the heavens and the earth, the sea, and all that is in them, but he rested on the seventh day. Therefore the Lord blessed the Sabbath day and made it holy.

Honour your father and your mother, so that you may live long in the land the Lord your God is giving you.

You shall not murder.

You shall not commit adultery.

You shall not steal.

You shall not give false testimony against your neighbour.

You shall not covet your neighbour's house. You shall not covet your neighbour's wife, or his male or female servant, his ox or donkey, or anything that belongs to your neighbour."

Exodus 20:1-17

Grace Upon Grace

Grace before law

"You yourselves have seen what I did to Egypt, and how I carried you on eagles' wings and brought you to myself. Now if you obey me fully and keep my covenant, then out of all nations you will be my treasured possession. Although the whole earth is mine, you will be for me a kingdom of priests and a holy nation."

Exodus 19:4-6

It's the story of the gospel: God rescues his people from slavery through the sacrificial blood of the lamb, to build them into a royal nation and a kingdom of priests, so that through them the whole world will see his glory.

And then he gives them the law.

The Old Testament law, of which the Ten Commandments stand at the beginning and as the foundation, was always given as an act of grace. Grace upon grace, coming as it did after God's gracious action of redeeming the Israelites from their slavery in Egypt. Grace upon grace shown towards the people he chose, not for anything that made them special, but simply because of his choice. It's perhaps because the writers understood the giving of the law as an act of grace that the Psalms contain expressions of deep love and appreciation for God's law (see Psalm 19:7-11, Psalm 119:107-114).

The ancient Israelites knew that they were not justified before God by their obedience, just as Christians do. Article 7 of the *Thirty-Nine Articles* states that, "The Old Testament is not contrary to the New: for both in the Old and New Testament everlasting life is offered to mankind by Christ." Salvation is, and has always been, by grace, through Christ.

What is the law for?

Laws don't make us perfectly obedient. When a teacher sets out the rules for their classroom, it doesn't mean that their students will never break those rules. When the government passes laws, it doesn't result in no criminal behaviour. Laws don't have that kind of power.

But laws and rules do establish an expected standard of behaviour. They reflect the values and priorities of the teacher in their classroom, or the government of a nation. Laws set the boundaries which will result in punishment or reward, so that we all know where we stand.   And, though they cannot perfectly control our behaviour, they do act as a deterrent. If we know that acting in a certain way will lead to a fine, or imprisonment, or detention, we are less likely to behave that way.

God's law works in the same ways. Traditionally, theologians have called this the "threefold use of the law": to be a mirror, a deterrent, and a standard for our behaviour.

How is God's law a mirror?

The law reflects the nature of God himself. The law shows us right from wrong as God sees it. It establishes his values and priorities in a way we can understand. The law also acts as a mirror for us. It shows us what we are really like, how far short of God's standards we fall. Without the law, we might persuade ourselves that we aren't too bad, really. We can find excuses for all kinds of sinful actions, but the law doesn't let us get away with those excuses.

How is God's law a deterrent?

God's law won't make us holy, but it can stop us from being as sinful as we could possibly be. There are both punishments and rewards on offer, and both are designed to change our behaviour to be more in line with God's will. Simply knowing God's standards ought to make us want to live accordingly. Similarly, when we are told that God finds a certain action detestable, that ought to motivate us to avoid it.

How is God's law a standard for our behaviour?

The law explains how to live lives that please our heavenly Father. God has not changed in the thousands of years since he gave his law and so his values, priorities, and standards have not changed, though of course we will need to think about how those apply at a different stage of salvation history. Christian freedom is freedom to love and obey our gracious, saving God, not freedom to indulge our sinful nature in any way we choose, and so we will still want to live up to his standards for our lives.

Jesus fulfilled the law

But surely Jesus came to fulfil the law, so that we don't have to? Well, not quite. What Jesus said was: "Do not think that I have come to abolish the Law or the Prophets; I have not come to abolish them but to fulfil them. For truly I tell you, until heaven and earth disappear, not the smallest letter, not the least stroke of a pen, will by any means disappear from the Law until everything is accomplished. Therefore anyone who sets aside one of the least of these commands and teaches others accordingly will be called least in the kingdom of heaven, but whoever practices and teaches these commands will be called great in the kingdom of heaven" (Matthew 5:17-19).

Jesus says that he came to fulfil the law but not to abolish it. The law remains until the last day, without the smallest dot being changed. So why don't we offer animal sacrifices anymore? And why are we happy to wear polycotton shirts and eat shellfish despite the Old Testament restrictions? Aren't we ignoring some laws while insisting on others?

The Old Testament law covers a wide range of different subjects, which Jesus fulfils in different ways. Let's go back to Article 7: "Although the law given by God through Moses is not binding on Christians as far as its forms of worship and ritual are concerned and the civil regulations are not binding on any nation state, nevertheless no Christian is free to disobey those commandments which may be classified as moral."

Jesus fulfilled the *ceremonial laws* concerning worship and ritual in a way that rendered them obsolete. There is no need for more sacrifices because Jesus has offered the one perfect sacrifice of himself, made once and for all. There is no need for more priests because Jesus is our great High Priest who has permanently opened the way for us into the most holy place. The ceremonial law has all been fulfilled in Christ and we keep it now simply through trusting in what he has done.

Jesus fulfilled the *civil law* by establishing the Kingdom of God which supersedes the nation of Israel. This means that some of these laws are no longer applicable, while others remain relevant in setting the principles for civil government. Laws needed for ordering and protecting an agricultural people in the Middle East don't always have direct application to industrialised societies in different parts of the world. Laws which distinguished the Israelites from their neighbours are no longer needed, since people of all nations have been gathered into God's kingdom. But, for example, the principles of justice established in the Old Testament law are still relevant in governing any nation in accordance with God's will.

The third category, which includes the Ten Commandments, is the moral law. Jesus fulfilled the *moral law* by his full obedience to it. In heart, mind, word, and deed, he loved his Father with all his strength, his mind, his heart, and will, and he loved his neighbour as himself. But he also says that whoever loves him will keep his commands. We are not excused obedience because of his. He is our example to copy, our leader to follow, our master to obey.

Questions for Reflection

1. Are you naturally a "rule breaker" or a "rule keeper"? What is your response to being told what to do?

2. What should motivate Christians to live holy lives?

3. In what ways are the Ten Commandments still relevant for Christians?

Prayer

Heavenly Father,
thank you for the gracious gift of your law.
Use it to teach us more of who you are,
to show us more of our sin,
and to lead us into greater godliness in everything we do.
Through Jesus Christ, our Lord,
Amen.

Remember Not to Forget

The first commandment

"And God spoke all these words: 'I am the LORD your God, who brought you out of Egypt, out of the land of slavery. You shall have no other gods before me.'"

Exodus 20:1-3

Imagine living in a world that was full of gods. A god of the sun and a god of the moon. A god for fire and a god for water. A god who could make the crops grow and another who could bless you with children. A god who demanded sacrifices and a god who kept changing his mind. Who would you worship? Who could you trust?

These days, we are accustomed to the idea that there is just one God, but the ancient world in which the Israelites lived was full of gods. In Egypt, where they had been enslaved for hundreds of years, the people worshipped many gods, some of which were benevolent and others not, some of which were associated with natural phenomena, and others which were associated with particular locations. In Canaan, the land which God was giving the Israelites, there were also many gods: gods with particular abilities such as warfare or healing; gods with complex myths surrounding them;

and gods who had to be kept happy.

But God, when he gives the first commandment to the Israelites, identifies himself clearly by his name and by his actions. There is no doubting which God this is.

He is the LORD. This is an English translation of the Hebrew word *Yahweh*, which older English Bibles wrote as Jehovah. Yahweh is the name God revealed to Moses (Exodus 3:14) and it asserts God's god-ness. It means something like, "I am who I am", implying that there is nothing and no one else God can be compared to. There is no other "god" who is like Yahweh. There is no other "god" who was not created. There is no other "god" who is eternal, all-powerful, all-knowing. There is no other "god" who is God.

Yahweh says, "You shall have no other gods before me." He does not mean that he is the "first among equals", leader of all the other gods, because there are no other gods. He means that the Israelites must not acknowledge any other gods at all. In God's presence, there is nothing and no one else to worship. There is nothing and no one else to trust. There is nothing and no one else to obey. There is only the Lord our God, who saved his people.

There is no other "god" who could save his people. The Israelites knew that to be true from their experience escaping from slavery in Egypt. How much more do we know that to be true from our experience of being saved from slavery to sin! The only God we are to acknowledge, the only God we are to worship, is the God whose name is Yahweh, the God who "has rescued us from the dominion of darkness and brought us into the kingdom of the Son he loves, in whom we have redemption, the forgiveness of sins" (Colossians 1:13-14).

In the introduction to the Ten Commandments we saw that there are three ways the law is important for Christians: as a mirror, a deterrent, and a standard.

A Mirror

As we have already seen, the first commandment shows us who God is: his name and his action. He is a God who saves. That is how we know who we mean by "God", we mean the God who saved us.

But the first commandment also holds up a mirror to us. It's shocking to think that the Israelites needed to be told to remember who God was and what he had done for them. Surely they wouldn't – couldn't – forget that in a hurry? And yet, before Moses even comes down the mountain, they have made an idol out of gold and begun to worship it in the very presence of God's holy mountain (Exodus 32).

We are no different to those Israelites. Given half a chance we will forget who God is and what he has done for us. Given the smallest temptation, we'll set our eyes on some other "god" which promises protection, fulfilment, or fun but which is no god at all.

A Deterrent

Don't get complacent. Don't assume that your faith will never waver or wander. Don't think you'll never forget who God is and what he has done. The commandment is there to remind you never to turn away to another "god", and it does so by reminding us who God is and what God has done.

How often do you remind yourself of the simple gospel by which you are saved? How often do you rejoice at what God has done in rescuing you? Do you ever look back at your own life to consider your personal history of God's salvation? *Remember*, the first commandment teaches us—remember not to forget!

A Standard

Faith doesn't come by looking inwardly at who we are or how we have changed. It comes by always looking up to God in heaven and back to God's saving actions in history. God himself is the reason for our worship and our obedience.

When Jesus was asked which was the greatest commandment, he had no hesitation in putting God first: "Love the Lord your God with all your heart and with all your soul and with all your mind." (Matthew 22:37). God first. God most. God above all.

> "I am the LORD your God, who brought you out of Egypt, out of the land of slavery. You shall have no other gods before me"
> (Exodus 20:1-3).

Questions for Reflection

1. Why do you think this is the first of the commandments?

2. How can you make sure you keep remembering not to forget what God has done for you?

3. What things are you tempted to trust or to worship before God?

Prayer

Almighty God,
thank you for saving your people
through the death and resurrection of the Lord Jesus Christ.
Help me never to forget who you are
and what you have done for me.
Guard me from the temptation
to trust and worship other gods before you
Amen.

Images of the Unimaginable

The second commandment

"You shall not make for yourself an image in the form of anything in heaven above or on the earth beneath or in the waters below. You shall not bow down to them or worship them; for I, the LORD your God, am a jealous God, punishing the children for the sin of the parents to the third and fourth generation of those who hate me, but showing love to a thousand generations of those who love me and keep my commandments."

Exodus 20:4-6

Have you ever tried to draw God? Or to imagine what he looks like? It's about as easy as trying to draw the whole universe on a postage stamp, or to imagine all the sub-atomic particles that make up your own body. It's not just hard, it's practically impossible!

One problem when we try to imagine what God is like is that we live within this physical world and we only know what things are like here. Try imagining a new colour outside the spectrum from red to purple. Or try imagining a scent you've never smelled. We can't do it. As created beings ourselves, our experience is limited to created things, and how could they possibly be like their Creator?

Because of this, people in many cultures around the world have represented the gods they worshipped in in physical forms that looked a bit like birds or animals or fish: things from the heavens above (skies), the earth beneath, or the waters below. But the Israelites were commanded not to make tangible images of God nor bow down and worship any such images.

It's important to be clear that the second commandment isn't a ban on art. This is about worship, not human creativity. The Israelites must not make any image which could take the place that is God's. They must not worship a created object, only the Creator God.

A Mirror

The Creator God cannot be represented by a created thing. While the creation speaks clearly of God's glory, wisdom, and power (Psalm 19:1-6), it does it so that we are prompted to worship the creator.

The second commandment also reflects several other important aspects of God's character. He is a jealous God, rightly wanting all that is due only to him. He will not stand idly by while we faithlessly dally with other objects of worship which distract us from him. He cannot tolerate sharing our favour with a worthless creation of our own hands. He is a God who will punish false worship.

He punishes the "children for the sin of the parents, even down to the third and fourth generation of those who hate me." Did you notice how God describes this sin? It's not a little thing. It's *hating* God. It's hating *God*. And the consequences of hating God are so serious that they cannot be contained within a single generation. Children, grandchildren, even great-grandchildren will all suffer because of this sin of their parents. God does not take sin lightly. He is a jealous God.

BUT... his love far outstrips his punishment. He will show love, not to three or four generations, but to a thousand generations of those who love him and obey his commands.

The second commandment also shows us what we are like. We do not often create physical objects of worship in modern Western society, but it has been rightly said that our hearts are "idol-factories." Our sinful hearts can find ways to make an idol of almost anything, tangible or intangible. Just like the Israelites, we take the good things which God has given us, and use them to forge our own golden calves. We lie to ourselves, as they did, pretending that it is just another way to worship God, when what we have really done is exchanged the true and living God with a lifeless, worthless idol.

A Deterrent

This commandment contains both warning and promise, a carrot and a stick. It warns us of the consequences of disobedience, and promises us the blessings of obedience.

The warning points out how serious our sin is and the consequences which will follow. Worshipping an idol is hating God. When we put anything else in God's place we provoke his jealous anger. Don't do it, the second commandment tells us! Don't bring his wrath down on yourself and your family. Don't take that risk!

Alongside the warning is the promise. Love him, and obey his commandments because you love him. Do what he says because you want to live in a way which pleases him. And if you do, you will rest secure in his love to a thousand generations.

A Standard

The second commandment shows us that God cares about how we worship him. The Israelites thought that a tangible "god" would help them to worship God better (Exodus 32:1-5), but God knew that they would worship the idol instead of him. While the first command is to worship the true God, the second is to worship him truly. The commandment doesn't leave us wondering what that means: love God and keep his commands. That is what God requires of us: love and obedience. God's standard for our behaviour is complete obedience. It sounds so simple, and it is.

In theory, anyway.

Questions for Reflection

1. Why do we find it easier to worship tangible objects than our heavenly God and Father?

2. Do you find the warning or the promise greater motivation to keep God's commands?

3. How can you keep your love for God and obedience to him growing every day?

Prayer

Almighty God,
creator of the heavens and the earth,
forgive us for the times when we set idols in your place.
Show us where we are worshipping your creation,
rather than you as our creator.
May we never provoke your jealous anger,
but rest secure in your love.
Teach us to love you more deeply
and obey you more completely every day,
Amen.

What's in a Name?

The third commandment

*"You shall not misuse the name of the LORD your God, for the
LORD will not hold anyone guiltless who misuses his name."*

Exodus 20:7

D o you ever swear? Maybe there are some words you'd
never say, and others you only use in certain situations.
But I wonder what you say when you miss the nail with
a hammer, or get an unexpected door in your face. We all have a
word we shout in anger, frustration, or pain, and for many people,
the words they turn to in those moments are words which ought
to be precious and holy, since they are the name of God himself.

Using God's name as a curse is an obvious example of misusing
it, but it is not the only one. The Heidelberg Catechism (a way of
explaining the faith, from the time of the Reformation) explains
that the third commandment means, "We are not to blaspheme
or to abuse the name of God by cursing, perjury, or unnecessary
oaths, nor to share in such horrible sins by being silent bystanders.
Rather, we must use the holy name of God only with fear and
reverence, so that we may rightly confess him, call upon him, and
praise him in all our words and works."

+ We misuse God's name if we blaspheme, that is if we speak
evil of God. If we say that God is a liar, if we say that God is

not all-powerful, if we say that God intended harm, if we say that God is no god at all, then we commit blasphemy.

+ We misuse God's name if we commit perjury, that is, telling a lie whilst under an oath we have sworn in God's name.

+ We misuse God's name if we make an unnecessary oath, that is a trivial or malicious oath, sworn in God's name.

+ We misuse God's name if we speak of him in any way that is not properly reverent, true, or appropriate.

A Mirror

The third commandment tells us that God's name is not to be trifled with, and by implication, that God himself is not to be trifled with. God is not a joking matter and God's name is not a punchline. The Lord our God is the eternal creator of the universe, the all-powerful saviour of his people. He is not a manmade deity to be invoked by a password or a catchphrase as if he were the genie in Aladdin's lamp. God alone is worthy of our worship, and his name should, therefore, be treated with due reverence.

This commandment holds up a mirror to us which makes one simple, stark judgment: guilty.

A Deterrent

The starkness of that judgment ought to make us think twice. Misusing God's name is a serious sin for which God will not hold us guiltless.

Why is this sin so serious? This sin matters because God's name represents God himself. When we misuse God's name, we abuse God himself. To use it as an expression of anger or pain is to call God the source of our anger and pain. To commit perjury in God's name is to call him a liar. To swear an unnecessary oath in his name is to cast doubt on his trustworthiness. To let others do so without speaking up is to admit that God does not matter to you.

So do not think that God doesn't care when someone misuses his name. Cursing and blasphemy were sins which carried the penalty of death (Leviticus 24:15-16). Be grateful for God's mercy shown to us in Christ, that we do not face the death penalty when we misuse God's name, but do not take that as license to keep sinning.

A Standard

One way to understand how we should keep this commandment is to look at how Christ fulfilled it and then follow his example. So, we may call God our Father, but we also call him Lord. We should speak to God as well as about God, but we ought not to do so casually, as if he were someone of no great importance. We should publicly declare our faith in him. We should plead with him in prayer, and bow before him in worship.

The third commandment demands more of us than controlling our tongues. Paul writes to Jews in Romans 2:23-24: "You who boast in the law, do you dishonour God by breaking the law? As it is written: 'God's name is blasphemed among the Gentiles because of you.'" When God's people behave in ways that dishonour God, it makes other people speak evil of God. Our lives need to be honouring to God, so that we give no one any excuse to break the third commandment.

Questions for Reflection

1. Why does God take this sin so very seriously?

2. Reflect on your own speech. Are there times when you use God's name, or the Lord Jesus Christ's name, irreverently or inappropriately?

3. How and when should you speak up against the misuse of God's name by other people?

Prayer

Almighty God,
thank you for teaching us your name and showing us yourself.
May we always hold your name in the highest honour,
defending it against all misuse.
Please forgive us for the times we have used
        your name inappropriately,
and teach us to speak about you more reverently
and to live in a manner that brings honour to your name,
Amen.

A Weekly Blessing

The fourth commandment

"Remember the Sabbath day by keeping it holy. Six days you shall labour and do all your work, but the seventh day is a sabbath to the LORD your God. On it you shall not do any work, neither you, nor your son or daughter, nor your male or female servant, nor your animals, nor any foreigner residing in your towns. For in six days the LORD made the heavens and the earth, the sea, and all that is in them, but he rested on the seventh day. Therefore the LORD blessed the Sabbath day and made it holy."

Exodus 20:8-11

"If you don't work, you don't eat", is a rule that still holds true for many people around the world, even if in our wealthy society most people are sheltered from that reality to some extent by the welfare state.

But the Sabbath always stood as a God-given exception to this rule. Keeping the Sabbath was an act of faith. It meant trusting that God would continue to provide for his people even if they did not work. Sabbath was a demonstration of grace: God provided for his people what they had not earned. The Sabbath year was an even more extreme example of this (Leviticus 25:1-7)—and the Israelites may never have had sufficient faith to put it into practice (2 Chronicles 36:21).

The commandment was to keep the Sabbath day holy. That is, to keep it separate, to keep it special. It was a day for the Lord, and not for the people. It was the day for the people to gather together (Leviticus 23:3) and a day to make offerings to God (Numbers 28:9-10).

Keeping the Sabbath holy involved resting. Six days to work and one to rest followed the pattern God set in making all creation. The seventh day was blessed by God and made holy. And so one important way of keeping the Sabbath holy was by resting from work. No one in the whole household was to work, not the servants, not the foreigners, not even the animals!

Finally, the Sabbath was a day for remembering what God had done. The Israelites were to remember how God had saved them out of slavery in Egypt (Deuteronomy 5:15). They were to tell each generation the stories of the plagues, the Passover, the escape through the Red Sea, the miraculous provision in the desert— over and over again. And yes, they were supposed to do this every day, but Sabbath provided a special opportunity to do so, free of all the normal chores of daily work.

A Mirror

The Sabbath reflects God's holiness. It is a holy day, set apart from the others, distinguished from them by its focus on God. God's holiness is illustrated for us in the way he sets aside holy times, holy places, holy objects, and holy things. Holy things must be separated from ordinary things. They must be kept special and different.

The commandment to keep a Sabbath reveals something about ourselves too. We are faithless people and we forget so quickly that we can and should trust God. We find it hard to trust that God will provide for us and our families. It is much easier to believe that we can do it ourselves. We need the weekly reminder that it is

God who provides for us. Having to stop work for one whole day every week is a tangible expression of our faith in God's gracious provision.

The command to keep the Sabbath holy reminds us that we need to keep our lives focussed on God. We need to meet with God's people, to make our freewill offerings to him, to be reminded of how God has saved us. One day a week is set aside for us to do those things, free from our normal responsibilities.

We're sometimes surprised how quickly the Israelites began complaining and groaning in the wilderness. How could they have forgotten God's amazing salvation so soon? But we are no different! We need reminding every week, because we can forget so easily.

A Deterrent

There is no explicit warning in the commandment, though we know that Sabbath-breaking was punishable by death (Numbers 15:32-36).

The commandment motivates obedience by giving us God's example to follow. If God himself worked for six days and then rested, who are we to think we can work for seven full days a week?

More even than that, we're told that God blessed the Sabbath. It is a gift he gives us, not a burden to be carried. A holy day, a special day, rest from daily work, a chance to gather together to hear once again the great story of God saving his people—what's not to love?

A Standard

The Sabbath commandment had civil and ceremonial aspects to it, as well as a moral aspect. Jesus fulfilled the ceremonial aspect of this law just as he did for the whole ceremonial law. We no longer need to make Sabbath sacrifices, for example. And we no longer live in a nation where Sabbath breaking could, or should, be punishable by law.

But as with all the commandments, when Jesus fulfilled the law, he did not abolish it. We still need to keep trusting that God will provide for us. We still need a constant, regular reminder of what God has done in saving us. We still need a time to gather together with God's people and offer ourselves to God. And we still need a day to rest from our work, because we are still not stronger than God who rested after all his work.

Christians don't keep Sabbath as the Israelites did, on the seventh day of the week. Instead we celebrate the instigation of the new kingdom through the resurrection of Christ on the *first* day of the week, that is, Sunday. But though the day has changed, and the ceremonial requirements are no longer relevant, we should not just throw out the fourth commandment. "The Sabbath was made for man, not man for the Sabbath" (Mark 2:27).

We still need the pattern of Sabbath-keeping that God has blessed us with, as we follow the example of Jesus, the Lord of the Sabbath.

Questions for Reflection

1. Why did God establish the Sabbath for his people?

2. In what ways has Jesus fulfilled the fourth commandment?

3. Why is it still important for Christians to keep a special day and a day of rest?

Prayer

Heavenly Father,
who provided miraculously for your people in the wilderness:
teach us to trust that you will provide for us.
May we gladly rest from all our work one day each week,
and make that day holy to God.
Let us never give up meeting with your people
to be reminded of our salvation in Christ.
Let us never forget what you have done for us in the past
and let us never give up hoping in the future Sabbath-rest
*   you have promised us,*
in Jesus's name,
Amen.

It's For Your Own Good

The fifth commandment

"Honour your father and your mother, so that you may live long in the land the LORD your God is giving you."

Exodus 20:12

Parents, huh? What do they know about anything? What do they know about living in the wilderness when they've spent their whole lives as slaves in Egypt? What do they know about the land God is giving the Israelites? They've never been there. Why should we listen to them?

Yours is not the first generation to question the wisdom of its parents. It's always been a temptation for children, and so God gave the children of the Old Testament wilderness generation this command to honour their parents. It's a command which is explicitly repeated in the New Testament: "Children, obey your parents in the Lord, for this is right. 'Honour your father and mother'— which is the first commandment with a promise—'so that it may go well with you and that you may enjoy long life on the earth.' Fathers, do not exasperate your children; instead, bring them up in the training and instruction of the Lord" (Ephesians 6:1-4).

Paul applies the commandment to children, in the context of

his longer discussion on the need for Christians to "submit to each other": wives to husbands, slaves to masters, and here, children to their parents. Obey your parents, he says, for this is right. Honouring involves obedience, and certainly this is true for children who are still members of their parents' household.

Honouring is not limited to obedience, though. Honouring an older parent means ensuring they are cared for and provided for (1 Timothy 5:3-8), for example. Honouring our parents means taking their wisdom to heart and applying it throughout our lives (Proverbs 1:8-9).

We live in a culture that places a high value on youth, and the appearance of youth. We're constantly being told how we can hide our grey hairs and smooth out our wrinkles. But the Bible has a different view: "Grey hair is a crown of splendour; it is attained in the way of righteousness" (Proverbs 16:31). We should respect age because with age comes experience and with experience comes wisdom.

And so, God tells the wilderness children to honour their parents so that they may have long lives in the promised land. They need their parents to make this journey, to share their wisdom, to lead each household. The promise is that the children will be blessed if they honour their parents. It's for their own good.

A Mirror

It's striking that the first commandment which is not directly about our relationship with God is about family. God made us to be in family units, to reflect something of his own nature as Father, Son, and Spirit. God cares about the relationship between parents and children because he is both Father and Son. The Son honours the Father. The Son obeys the Father. The Son is blessed because he glorifies his Father.

Our family relationships are supposed to reflect God's family relationship. But we don't have to look very far to see families that are broken. It's not just marriages that are broken, though that is sadly true. Whole family units are scattered, separated and estranged, hating and hurting. Siblings are rivals. Children wilfully disobey their parents, disrespect them, and abandon them to be cared for by strangers. Sin messes up families in every way imaginable. Yours and mine included.

A Deterrent

Again we have a commandment with a promise, rather than a warning. The promise is for long life in the land God is giving them. That was everything they were hoping for: a new place, a new life, long and prosperous. God says it will be theirs, if only they will honour their parents.

Obey your parents because it is the right thing to do, says Paul. The promise is a good, if perhaps somewhat selfish, motivation. But we ought to do it just because it is right, just because God tells us. If we want to obey our heavenly Father, we will honour our earthly parents.

A Standard

This is where the rubber hits the road: how should we honour our parents?

It's going to look different at different times in our lives: for young children, for teenagers, for adult children who are now living in their own households, for those caring for elderly parents, and so on. At times it will mean obedience, even if we disagree, whereas at other times it may mean listening and respecting before making our own choices. It will always mean being careful not to demean, belittle, or disrespect our parents.

Honouring parents who are not Christians is likely to involve more disagreement, but should not mean less respect. We'll want to share the gospel with them, but we'll need to be careful not to dishonour their role in our lives as we do so. Honouring parents who have mistreated or abused their children may involve difficult decisions about limiting contact and telling hard truths. We do not have a license to exaggerate or to exact revenge, even when our parents have not treated us as they should. Honouring elderly parents may mean arranging the professional care that they need, but it won't mean abandoning them to the professionals. It may mean continuing to love them even when they no longer know us, just as they loved us when we were tiny babies who did not know them.

Honour your heavenly Father, by honouring your earthly parents, so that it may go well with you in the land God is giving you.

Questions for Reflection

1. What do you find hardest about your relationship with your parents?

2. Why should Christians seek to honour their parents?

3. Can you think of practical ways you could honour your parents more?

Prayer

Almighty God, our heavenly Father,
thank you for calling us into your eternal family
and placing us in our families here on earth.
Teach us how to honour our parents,
to love them and listen to their wisdom,
to care for them and provide for them, as they need.
Help us to forgive past wrongs
and seek peace within our families, for Jesus's sake,
Amen.

Every Life Matters

The sixth commandment

"You shall not murder."

Exodus 20:13

I s that a little sigh of relief I can hear? Finally we get to a commandment most of us feel pretty sure we can keep. Maybe you know that you haven't always honoured your parents, and that you sometimes misuse God's name. But at least you've never murdered anyone.

Except, of course, some people have. And if that's you, it's very important that you know God can forgive you, through Christ, no matter what you have done. Christians aren't just the "good guys", the people who keep up appearances and never have a run in with the law. Christians are the bad guys, the sinners, of all kinds and in all ways, who have recognised their sin and turned to Christ in repentance and faith.

This commandment, together with the ones that follow it, doesn't have any explanation, promise, or warning. It should be obvious why it's wrong and it should be clear to us why God commands us not to do it. Life is precious. Life is given by God. Only God has the right, therefore, to take a life away. There is a moral imperative here. It's not just a law given to keep Israelite society functioning well. Life matters to God and therefore life should matter to us.

In English law, we distinguish between several different kinds of killing: murder, manslaughter, killing in self-defence, killing as a soldier in war and so on. The Hebrew word used in the sixth commandment means more than just what we would call murder. It's about taking the law into your own hands, killing someone without the authority of the state behind you. Accidental killing was recognised as something different and provision was made to protect accidental killers in the cities of refuge (Numbers 35:6-32).

Murder polluted the whole community, even the land on which they lived: "Do not pollute the land where you are. Bloodshed pollutes the land, and atonement cannot be made for the land on which blood has been shed, except by the blood of the one who shed it. Do not defile the land where you live and where I dwell, for I, the Lord, dwell among the Israelites" (Numbers 35:33-34).

A Mirror

God is the lifegiver. He breathed life into Adam and he breathes life into each one of us: "he himself gives everyone life and breath and everything else" (Acts 17:25). God is the sustainer of all life: "For in him we live and move and have our being" (Acts 17:28).

And so, to take a life is to set ourselves up directly against God. Killing someone takes away the life that God has given and God has sustained. He is the lifegiver and we must not be lifetakers. More than that, since life is a gift from God and life is precious to God, we should do whatever we can to preserve life.

A Deterrent

Did the Israelites really need to be told that murder was wrong? Do we really need God to point that out to us? Surely we all have enough of an inherent sense of morality to have worked that out for ourselves? Well, yes and no.

It's true that in pretty much every human society the act of deliberately taking someone else's life is reckoned as wrong. Or at least in some contexts it is, even if in some circumstances it is permitted. But as we saw earlier, the sixth commandment isn't only speaking about the kinds of killing that our courts would reckon as murder. Killing in revenge, killing by negligence, killing under the guise of medical intervention are all prohibited.

We don't just have a responsibility not to take life; we also have a duty to prevent lives being taken in any and all of these ways, insofar as we are able. That means speaking out against euthanasia and abortion. But it also means being careful in the way that we drive and ensuring that health and safety guidelines are kept in our workplaces. It means giving generously to people who don't have access to food or medical care. It means teaching our children that every person's life matters to God.

A Standard

Jesus said, "You have heard that it was said to the people long ago, 'You shall not murder, and anyone who murders will be subject to judgment.' But I tell you that anyone who is angry with a brother or sister will be subject to judgment. Again, anyone who says to a brother or sister, 'Raca,' is answerable to the court. And anyone who says, 'You fool!' will be in danger of the fire of hell" (Matthew 5:21-22).

Jesus shows us that the standard set by the sixth commandment is far higher than we might have first thought. It's not just those who pull the trigger or drive the knife in who will be judged under this command. It's "anyone who is angry with a brother or sister." It's anyone who calls names and mocks with insults. It's anyone who hates in their hearts whether or not they take action with their hands.

It's you and me.

Questions for Reflection

1. How have you broken the sixth commandment?

2. Why is human life so precious?

3. What actions could you take to help protect lives?

Prayer

Almighty God, the giver of life,
who sustains us through every breath,
may we never take the gift of life for granted.
Lord Jesus, we are sorry for all the times we have
committed murder in our hearts
by our anger and mockery.
Please show us how we can do more
to protect and preserve the lives of others,
for your glory,
Amen.

Don't be Seduced by Sex

The seventh commandment

"You shall not commit adultery."

Exodus 20:14

W hy are Christians obsessed with sex? Surely what happens in someone's bedroom is none of anyone else's business?

Certainly we should notice that of the Ten Commandments only one is explicitly concerned with sex (though the tenth commandment also has relevance), and it's by no means at the top of the list. God's commands are concerned with the whole of life, and we should be careful not to make it seem as though our sex lives are the only things that matter to God.

Nevertheless, God is concerned with our sex lives. Here he commands the Israelites not to commit adultery. Later in the law, this command is expanded so that it is not just about extra-marital affairs. The Israelites must not commit incest, must not commit rape, must not commit bestiality, and must not have sex with people of the same sex (Leviticus 18).

Why does God care? First, because God cares about families. God created human beings to be in family units: a man, his wife, their children (Genesis 2:24). God established his special people, the Israelites as a family unit (Genesis 15:4-5). The family unit, as we have already seen, is a reflection of God himself: Father, Son, and Spirit.

But adultery breaks up family units. Incest devastates the normal order of family life. Rape is a travesty of the sexual love that should seal a marriage. Bestiality is a clear perversion of the family unit. And homosexual sex cannot be the foundation for a family.

Second, because sex is a God-given gift, and like all of God's gifts, it is best enjoyed in the way the maker intended. He does not give rules about when and with whom to have sex in order to limit our enjoyment, but in order to maximise it.

For the Israelites, this attitude to sex would have set them apart from the nations around them. Prostitution, rape, adultery, incest, and homosexual sex were part of the culture at that time, just as they are today. God wanted his people to act differently. God still wants his people to act differently.

A Mirror

The Bible teaches us that our relationship with God is like a marriage. There is a period of courtship and betrothal, and a covenant promise, followed by faithless adultery on the part of the Israelites, while God was always faithful to his people.

And so God sent the bridegroom himself, Christ, to win his bride by laying down his life for her. As Christians, we are living in anticipation of the wedding day and the consummation of that relationship. Sex is the nearest human experience to the joy and love we will experience when we are together with Christ.

Sex is not something we should mess around with. It's not something we can try out in any way we feel like. God didn't invent sex primarily for our immediate enjoyment, but to teach us what it is we have to look forward to. It will only do that if we're having sex in the way that God established. Our faithfulness to God should be matched by our faithfulness in marriage.

A Deterrent

Sex is tempting. Sex is seductive. Sex promises so much. Sex lies and tells us that it does no harm. We need to be told that adultery is wrong because we are so easily deceived into thinking that it is okay. We need to be reminded that God hates adultery because he is always faithful.

We need to see that God loves families and adultery devastates families. We need to recognise the destruction that can be caused by sex in the wrong time, with the wrong person, in the wrong context. You shall not commit adultery.

A Standard

Jesus said, "You have heard that it was said, 'You shall not commit adultery.' But I tell you that anyone who looks at a woman lustfully has already committed adultery with her in his heart" (Matthew 5:27-28).

Once again Jesus raises the bar. Not merely sexual activity, but sexual desire can count as adultery. What does it mean to look at someone lustfully? It means to want them, to fantasise about them, to be undressing them in your mind. I don't think it means simply acknowledging someone's attractiveness, but I do think it can be an easy step from admiration to lust.

Our society makes that step very, very easy indeed. Both men and women are depicted in adverts, on TV, and in films in overtly sexual ways. Even children are regularly exposed to sexual content online and in social media. Our standards of what is acceptable are constantly changing, based on the world around us. But God's standards do not change.

Keeping the seventh commandment won't always be easy. It will set us apart from other people. It will make us look weird and prudish. Sometimes we'll mess up. Sometimes we'll be seduced into believing the lies. Sometimes we'll know what we're doing is wrong and do it anyway.

That's when we'll need to repent and be forgiven: "Do not be deceived: Neither the sexually immoral nor idolaters nor adulterers nor men who have sex with men nor thieves nor the greedy nor drunkards nor slanderers nor swindlers will inherit the kingdom of God. And that is what some of you were. But you were washed, you were sanctified, you were justified in the name of the Lord Jesus Christ and by the Spirit of our God" (1 Corinthians 6:9-11).

Questions for Reflection

1. How are God's rules about sex designed to maximise enjoyment rather than limit it?

2. Why do we need this commandment?

3. What do you need to repent of and seek God's forgiveness for?

Prayer

Loving Father, thank you for your good and gracious laws
which teach us the best way to live in your world.
Forgive us, Lord,
for the ways in which we have failed to meet your standards.
Please guard us and guide us by your Holy Spirit
as we seek to be faithful to you in our sexuality,
in Jesus's name,
Amen.

Be Content With That

The eighth commandment

"You shall not steal."

Exodus 20:15

Y ou know what it's like. Your family rushed out of Egypt, leaving everything behind like they were supposed to. But Dan's family over there, well, they planned ahead and filled their backpacks with all kinds of things. So now he's got a new pair of leather sandals and he doesn't even want his old ones. Yours have been in bits for months. I mean, he's not even using them. He probably wouldn't even notice. They're just there. Lying at the door of his tent. You could just try them on for size…

Moses calls you all to the mountain. There's thunder and lightning and it's absolutely terrifying. And God speaks. He's telling everyone what it's going to mean for him to be in charge. There's a list of rules. He gets to the eighth, and it's like he's speaking directly to you: "You shall not steal."

You shall not steal. Don't do it. You glance over at Dan. He's looking up the mountain to where God is. You glance down at your sandals. You could probably fix them so they last for another month or two. And then Dan looks at you and smiles. And when you come down the mountain he runs over, takes the new sandals off his feet and offers them to you. "Here," he says. "Take these. I have more than I need and I want you to have them."

Don't steal, God says. Haven't I given you enough? Don't you trust me to keep providing everything you need? Even here, in the wilderness, haven't I given you water and food, and everything you've needed to survive?

This is the LORD, your God, who brought you out of slavery. This is the God who has called you his own. This is the God who has given you everything. So why would you ever need to take more?

A Mirror

This commandment is a reminder that everything we have comes from God. Everything we need, everything we enjoy, everything we think of as our own has its origin in God the creator and the provider. God is generous and gracious, giving us more than we need and more than we deserve.

And yet we are always wanting more. Like the Israelites complaining in the desert, we are never content with what God has given us. We're never satisfied. We constantly want what we do not have. We're always jealous of people who seem to have more. And if we think we can get away with it, we'll be tempted to take what does not belong to us.

A Deterrent

Don't do it, says God. Don't steal.

First, remember that even if you think you can get away with it, God will see. God will know.

Second, remember that sins never stay secret. The sin of stealing is one that breaks trust and harms communities. See Joshua 7 for one story from Israel's history that shows how one man's theft brought defeat to the whole people.

Third, remember that stealing is not just a sin against another person. It is a sin against God. Stealing is saying to God that we don't trust him to give us everything we need. Stealing is denying God's gracious generosity to us. Instead, learn to trust him more. Learn to be content with what he has given you.

A Standard

We didn't even need to wait for Jesus to explain how this commandment should be applied. John the Baptist was able to tell his followers: "Anyone who has two shirts should share with the one who has none, and anyone who has food should do the same." Even tax collectors came to be baptised. "Teacher," they asked, "what should we do?" "Don't collect any more than you are required to," he told them. Then some soldiers asked him, "And what should we do?" He replied, "Don't extort money and don't accuse people falsely—be content with your pay" (Luke 3:10-14).

The eighth commandment implies more than just not taking other people's things. It sets a standard for honest dealings and generosity towards others. Share with those who need it, because sometimes the way God provides for our needs is through the generosity of others. Don't be dishonest at work, taking what isn't rightfully yours. Don't defraud people, don't bring false claims.

There are all kinds of subtle and not-subtle ways we can steal what is not ours. Wasting work time checking our Facebook and Twitter pages. Helping ourselves to more than our fair share of family resources. Not being completely honest in the way we describe items we're selling. Greedily demanding the best of everything on offer. Failing to declare all our income to Her Majesty's Revenue and Customs. Not giving generously to share with those who are in need. There are a hundred other ways to break this commandment without ever doing anything illegal.

Learn to be content with what you have, generous in how you

share with others, and not to put your trust in money and material possessions. As Paul says, "But godliness with contentment is great gain. For we brought nothing into the world, and we can take nothing out of it. But if we have food and clothing, we will be content with that. Those who want to get rich fall into temptation and a trap and into many foolish and harmful desires that plunge people into ruin and destruction. For the love of money is a root of all kinds of evil. Some people, eager for money, have wandered from the faith and pierced themselves with many griefs" (1 Timothy 6:6-10).

Questions for Reflection

1. Do you think of yourself as rich or poor? Why?

2. How does your attitude to money and possessions reflect your attitude to God?

3. How can you be more generous with what God has given you?

Prayer

Gracious God,
thank you for your generous provision
of everything we need and more.
Teach us to be content with what we have
and generous in sharing it with others.
May we never be tempted to wander from the faith by love of money,
but always keep trusting you, our Saviour and Provider,
for we ask in Jesus's name,
Amen.

Truth and Justice

The ninth commandment

"You shall not give false testimony against your neighbour."

Exodus 20:16

H ave you ever been accused of something you didn't do? Perhaps a teacher assumed wrongly that you were involved in causing trouble. Maybe your parents sometimes jumped to false conclusions. Or, more seriously, you might have been legally charged with a crime you didn't commit.

It's a horrible thing when it happens. We rightly rush to defend ourselves, to provide evidence that we're innocent, to speak up against the accusations. But even if we can prove that we didn't do it, the whole thing leaves a bitter taste. Why were people so quick to believe wrong of us? Don't they know us better than that?

A false accusation is always hurtful and unpleasant. A false accusation made deliberately is much, much worse. When your brother lies to your parents, telling them he saw you break that plate. When someone you thought was your friend goes telling lies to a teacher, so that you get stuck with a detention you've done nothing to deserve. When a person stands up in court and gives false testimony condemning you.

That's not just a lie. That's a lie which damages lives, breaks relationships, and destroys society. That's a lie whose victim is justice itself. And without justice, there is anarchy.

God tells the Israelites that they must not give false testimony, not only because he cares about truth, but also because he cares about justice. Their society is to be built on truth and justice, because their nation is to bear witness to God himself.

A Mirror

This commandment reflects those two fundamental aspects of God's character: truth and justice.

> "God is not human, that he should lie,
>   not a human being, that he should change his mind.
> Does he speak and then not act?
> Does he promise and not fulfil?" (Numbers 23:19)

God's honesty is absolute. He cannot lie. He does not break promises. He will not bear false witness. God is a judge who will always judge justly. He knows all the evidence. He is not deceived by false testimony. His justice is absolute.

But we are human beings and we do lie, change our mind, break our promises. First the serpent, then Eve, and finally Adam, distorted God's words to them in the garden. Twisting the truth, not telling the whole truth, and abandoning the truth altogether, the devil is the "father of lies" (John 8:44), and our sinful nature makes us like him.

A Deterrent

Exodus 23 expands on this commandment, showing us why it is such a serious matter:

> "Do not spread false reports. Do not help a guilty person by being a malicious witness. Do not follow the crowd in doing wrong. When you give testimony in a lawsuit, do not pervert

justice by siding with the crowd, and do not show favouritism to a poor person in a lawsuit. If you come across your enemy's ox or donkey wandering off, be sure to return it. If you see the donkey of someone who hates you fallen down under its load, do not leave it there; be sure you help them with it. Do not deny justice to your poor people in their lawsuits. Have nothing to do with a false charge and do not put an innocent or honest person to death, for I will not acquit the guilty. Do not accept a bribe, for a bribe blinds those who see and twists the words of the innocent. Do not oppress a foreigner; you yourselves know how it feels to be foreigners, because you were foreigners in Egypt"
(Exodus 23:1-9).

Why might we be tempted to bear false witness or act unjustly? Exodus 23 suggests:

- Malicious spite.
- Peer pressure.
- Favouritism.
- Hatred.
- Wealth.
- Bribery.
- Racism.

It's an ugly list, isn't it? Injustice is an ugly thing, arising from ugly motives. The lie may seem a small thing. It may feel easy as it slips out of your mouth. But the lie is always a symptom of a darkened, sinful heart.

Don't bear false testimony because it's yourself that you will condemn.

A Standard

The commandment tells us not to bear false testimony against our neighbour. We know who our neighbour is, as Jesus illustrated so powerfully in the parable of the Good Samaritan (Luke 10:25-

37): everyone. God's standards of truthfulness and justice must be applied across the board.

Paul tells the Colossians that lying is incompatible with being a Christian:

> "But now you must also rid yourselves of all such things as these: anger, rage, malice, slander, and filthy language from your lips. Do not lie to each other, since you have taken off your old self with its practices and have put on the new self, which is being renewed in knowledge in the image of its Creator. Here there is no Gentile or Jew, circumcised or uncircumcised, barbarian, Scythian, slave or free, but Christ is all, and is in all."
>
> (Colossians 3:8-11)

As we become more and more like our heavenly Father, we cannot continue to imitate the father of lies. As we are joined into God's family, we cannot continue to show prejudice to some of that family. There is no difference: Jew or Gentile, slave or free, male or female, rich or poor, black or white. Christ is all and is in all.

Questions for Reflection

1. Why does God give this commandment?

2. Look at the list of reasons given in Exodus 23 for bearing false witness. Which do you find hardest to resist?

3. What steps could you take to work positively towards truth and justice in your community?

Prayer

God of all justice,
who sees and knows all truth:
forgive us for our deceitfulness and injustice.
As those who are being renewed in your image,
make us honest and just in all our dealings.
May we be known as people who are trustworthy and fair,
bearing witness to your truth and justice,
for the sake of Jesus—the way, the truth, and the life,
Amen.

Inside and Out

The tenth commandment

"You shall not covet your neighbour's house. You shall not covet your neighbour's wife, or his male or female servant, his ox or donkey, or anything that belongs to your neighbour."

Exodus 20:17

Imagine you were an Israelite standing at the foot of Mount Sinai, listening to the Ten Commandments. At what point would you start to worry that this was a list of laws you could not keep? I guess it would depend how well you know yourself and how fully you understood what these laws required from you. But perhaps you might have thought that it was possible to manage the first three commandments: how could anything take the place of the God who saved you and why would you ever want to misuse his name or worship him wrongly? And as the list went on: you've always loved and honoured your parents, you think a day of rest sounds wonderful, and you're a decent person: murder, theft, adultery, false witness all sound like things you'd never dream of doing.

But then God tells you not to covet. Suddenly that's a whole different level of obedience. Because this is the only commandment which is specifically about our thoughts. The previous commandments do have implications for our thoughts as well as our actions, but there is no action associated with coveting. It is a state of mind, a thought. It's internal, not external.

Keeping control of your thoughts is much, much harder than keeping control of your actions. And coveting is a particularly dangerous way of thinking.

Coveting doesn't involve taking someone else's stuff, but it is about wanting someone else's stuff. Or their animals. Or their servants. Or their spouse. If we want something, we will be tempted to take it, and so coveting can lead to stealing.

But you aren't a thief, so you don't take it. Instead, you start to envy the person it does belong to. Envy can lead to resentment, resentment can lead to anger, and anger can lead to murder.

But you aren't a murderer, so you keep your envy hidden. It's hard when you see your neighbour's wife every day. His very beautiful wife. And you start to wonder what it would be like to kiss her. To touch her. To have sex with her. Coveting your neighbour's wife can lead to lust, and lust can lead to adultery.

But you aren't an adulterer, so you go back inside and dismiss her from your mind. Only you know she would make you happy. She would give you everything you need to be satisfied. But only God can satisfy and we should find all our delight in him. You've started to think about her the way you should only be thinking about God. Covetousness is idolatry (Colossians 3:5).

Coveting is a dangerous way of thinking. It's sinful in itself and it leads to all kinds of other sins.

A Mirror

God is not envious or covetous. God is a jealous God, not an envious God. That is, he wants what is rightfully his, not what is rightfully someone else's. He doesn't want anything that belongs to someone else, because the world and everything in it already belongs to him.

Our sinful nature is always making us greedily look out for

things that aren't ours so that we wish they were. Covetousness means looking at the world and everything in it... and wanting it. And so the tenth commandment shows us the heart of our sin: wanting to be God.

A Deterrent

If the Israelites hadn't been given this commandment, they might have thought that only their external behaviour mattered to God. They might have thought it would be enough to stop themselves from acting on their sinful thoughts.

But God requires us to be good on the inside. God's standards are infinitely higher than anyone else's. It doesn't matter if other people see us doing lots of good things and think that we're good people. God knows what we are like in our heads and our hearts, and so the tenth commandment prompts us to change our thinking and our emotions. We don't have to let our sinful nature take charge. We have the Spirit of God in us, transforming us, helping us to change from the inside.

A Standard

Jesus said, "But those things which proceed out of the mouth come from the heart, and they defile a man. For out of the heart proceed evil thoughts, murders, adulteries, fornications, thefts, false witness, blasphemies. These are the things which defile a man" (Matthew 15:18-20). Don't let your mind be taken over by covetous thoughts. As Jesus says, our actions spring out of our thoughts.

What can you do to stop thinking this way? How do we "take every thought captive for Christ" (2 Corinthians 10:5)?

+ Pray! Ask God to help you control your thoughts.

+ Practice! Plan and practice what you will do when you start to covet something.

- Be aware! Notice when you are coveting something that isn't yours.

- Stop! Tell yourself that you don't want to think that way.

- Change! Make a conscious effort to think about something else. Perhaps memorise a Bible verse for this situation, or pray for the person whose belongings you are coveting.

It'll be hard work at first, but it will get easier and the Holy Spirit will help you. It's his job to make us more and more like Christ each day.

The Ten Commandments

> "When the people saw the thunder and lightning and heard the trumpet and saw the mountain in smoke, they trembled with fear. They stayed at a distance and said to Moses, 'Speak to us yourself and we will listen. But do not have God speak to us or we will die.' Moses said to the people, 'Do not be afraid. God has come to test you, so that the fear of God will be with you to keep you from sinning.' The people remained at a distance, while Moses approached the thick darkness where God was."
>
> (Exodus 20:18-21)

The giving of the ten commandments was terrifying for the Israelites. They knew God as their saviour, but that did not make them complacent in his presence. Moses tells them not to be afraid, but also that the fear of God would keep them from sinning.

As Christians, we too know that we do not need to be afraid of God, but that should not make us complacent in his presence. God is awesome and terrifying, he is all-powerful and all-knowing, and he cares about what we do and how we think. The fear of God should keep us from sinning.

Questions for Reflection

1. Why is it so dangerous to covet things which are not ours?

2. Is it more difficult to be obedient to God in your thoughts or your actions? Why?

3. Read through all of the ten commandments. How should Christians respond to these words of God?

Prayer

Almighty God,
the world and everything in it is yours.
Help us to be grateful for what we have
and glad for others when they have more.
Please guard our hearts and minds from covetousness,
and teach us that true satisfaction and delight are found only in you.
Lord, we know that we are sinners, inside and out.
Thank you for sending the Lord Jesus to die for sinners,
         once-and-for-all,
to bring us into relationship with you.
May our salvation never make us complacent,
but rather add grace upon grace
by transforming our lives in obedience to your law,
by the power of your Holy Spirit,
Amen.

The Lord's Prayer

"One day Jesus was praying in a certain place. When he finished, one of his disciples said to him, 'Lord, teach us to pray, just as John taught his disciples.'

He said to them, 'When you pray, say:
Father, hallowed be your name,
your kingdom come.
Give us each day our daily bread.
Forgive us our sins,
 for we also forgive everyone who sins against us.
And lead us not into temptation.'"

Luke 11:1-5

"This, then, is how you should pray:

Our Father in heaven, hallowed be your name,
 your kingdom come, your will be done,
on earth as it is in heaven.
Give us today our daily bread.
And forgive us our debts,
as we also have forgiven our debtors.
And lead us not into temptation,
but deliver us from the evil one."

Matthew 6:9-13

A Model Prayer

The Lord's Prayer will be familiar to anyone of a certain generation schooled in England and other parts of the world, and certainly to anyone who has spent any time in an Anglican church. It may be the most often repeated piece of Scripture of them all.

But why is it so well known? After all, it is not Jesus's only prayer. We are told repeatedly that Jesus prayed, and we are given insight into his prayer life at Gethsemane (Luke 22:42), at the cross (Luke 23:34), and in his High Priestly Prayer (John 17). In fact, the Lord's Prayer is not a prayer by Jesus at all. It is, rather, a gift from Jesus to his Church. In Luke's version, Jesus is responding to the request of his disciples: "Lord, teach us to pray" (Luke 11:1) and in Matthew's account, it is part of his wider teaching in the Sermon on the Mount (Matthew 6:5-15).

This is not everything that Jesus wants to say on prayer, either. Earlier in the Sermon, Jesus tells us to pray for those who persecute you (Matthew 5:44). This is not everything that Jesus has to say, and certainly not everything that the Bible would want us to know about prayer.

But it is a model prayer. Indeed, it is *the* model prayer; a prayer from Jesus for his Church to use in relating to their heavenly Father. The prayer is familiar to us because it features in every Holy Communion service and every Service of the Word in the Church of England. This is the prayer that Jesus taught us and it has become the prayer that the Church uses, often.

It may be helpful at this point to pay attention to the context of the prayer before we think about how we can use it for ourselves to best effect.

Matthew's account

The Lord's Prayer falls right in the middle of the Sermon on the Mount. Jesus begins to address prayer, as a part of the wider narrative on Christian living, with the words "And when you pray" because, for Jesus, prayer is a given (Matthew 6:5). The Lord's Prayer is not about encouraging us to pray, but to pray for the right reasons and in the right way.

Jesus knows that the church of his day is full of hypocrites. They seek the approval of others and so they make all their prayers public: "they love to pray standing on the street corners to be seen by others." And they will be seen: "Truly I tell you, they have received their reward in full" (Matthew 6:5). It is possible to use the right forms and words of prayer, but have no thought of God in your heart, if all you want is that others think of you as a religious person.

The answer is not to give up prayer altogether, nor to give up corporate prayer. The answer is to make sure you also "go into your room, close the door and pray to your Father" (Matthew 6:6). It is the Father to whom we pray, and it is the Father who rewards our prayers with his gracious answers. We should pray for the right reasons.

But equally, we must pray in the right way. Jesus does pray longer prayers than this (see John 17), but he urges us not to "keep on babbling like pagans, for they think they will be heard because of their many words" (Matthew 6:7). The pagans pray long prayers because they think that God has to take notice of the prayer the longer it is. Not so, says Jesus. An arrow prayer, a single word, is enough to get the attention of a gracious Father. Moreover, the "Father knows what you need before you ask him" (Matthew 6:8). God is not ignorant, needing a shopping list from us before he knows what to do. Our Father knows our situation better than we know it ourselves.

In other words, our prayers are an expression of our dependence on him, not an attempt to twist his arm, or inform him of things he doesn't understand.

Matthew's Gospel teaches us we must pray to God, not to people, and that we must pray as though he were God, and not some impotent pagan deity.

Luke's account

Luke gives us an even briefer account of the prayer in his Gospel, as though emphasising the point Matthew makes about not babbling. Again, the disciples in Luke assume they will pray. Jesus teaches them what to pray, but then gives them great encouragement to persevere in prayer. Jesus follows the prayer with the story of the man who asks a neighbour for bread to feed a traveller who has just arrived. Not because the cause is good, but because of the man's "shameless audacity" the neighbour relents (Luke 11:5-8). Then he tells the story of the father who, despite being evil, knows that if his son asks for an egg he should not give him a scorpion, nor a stone for a loaf of bread (Luke 11:11-12). In both cases, the principle is this: if this is how it works in human relationships, *how much more generous* will God be. For God is a Father to his people, but not an evil one. He will give the Holy Spirit in fulfilment of the prayer if we ask (Luke 11:13). And we should ask because "it will be given", because our God is a generous God.

How shall we approach the Lord's Prayer?

What the Gospel accounts of the Lord's Prayer remind us is that the prayer is devotional before it is liturgical. That is, it is right and proper that the Church should have such a model prayer in her liturgy. But Jesus teaches us to pray in private. It is a devotional prayer. It is first of all about you and your walk with your heavenly Father.

Matthew tells us that God rewards those who pray. Luke tells us that God is generous to those who ask. So both Gospels teach us dependence. We are to depend on God for everything that we need. Of course, the prayer itself will teach us what those things are that we need. So, perhaps the thing that the following chapters offer us is an encouragement to pray consistently and persistently to our heavenly Father, in private, for those things he is willing to give according to the prayer Jesus taught us.

Questions for Reflection

1. Where do you pray most, in public or in private?

2. What do you most often pray about?

3. What motivates you to pray?

Prayer

Our Father,
make us people of prayer.
Help me to know that you are a gracious Father who answers prayer.
Though my lips are stumbling,
and I often do not know what to pray,
thank you that you accept simple prayers and long to reward them.
Please grant that I may learn how to pray
in line with your will.
In the name of Jesus Christ, our Lord,
Amen.

An Outrageous Prayer

"Our Father in heaven, hallowed be your name."

Matthew 6:9, Luke 11:2

One year, I had the privilege of reading through Mark's Gospel with some of the children from church. When we got to Mark 3:6, where we are told that "the Pharisees went out and began to plot with the Herodians how they might kill Jesus," there was uproar: "They can't do that!" The beauty of seeing them encounter that text for the first time reminded me that sometimes familiarity makes us too comfortable with the more outrageous aspects of the Gospels.

The opening line of the Lord's Prayer is just one such outrage.

Consider for a moment how Roman Catholics are encouraged to pray. They call on the saints and on Mary to be their intercessors with God. They know that they are unworthy to call on the great God who dwells in heaven, so they look for a more lowly mediator. But Jesus commands his people to speak directly to God.

Yet the real outrage of the prayer is *how* we are to address God. We are to approach him as *Father*. Indeed, the word has the sense of more intimacy than this. Not quite "Daddy", but not far off.

This is the relationship that Jesus has had with his Father from all eternity. In the Sermon on the Mount, Jesus teaches us how to live to "glorify your Father in heaven" (Matthew 5:20), and reminds us to "be perfect, therefore, as your heavenly Father is perfect" (Matthew 5:48). In fact, we are to orientate our lives so that our rewards come from our Father in heaven, and not from men (Matthew 6:1). Jesus characterises the whole Christian life as a relationship with our Father in heaven, and so it is no surprise that we should address him as our Father.

We should not rush past this without considering what it cost. It cost Jesus his perfect life, in the place of our wicked ones, as our substitute to bring us back into that relationship with the Father, by adoption.

Of course, it is helpful in our individualistic age to notice that Jesus taught each one to pray *Our* Father. As we saw in the previous chapter, this is a prayer for your bedroom as much as for church, and yet it is still a corporate prayer. As the Father's adoptive children, we share not only an intimacy with him, but also with each other. Now the burdens of one person become the burdens of all, and so we are to pray not only for ourselves but for God's people everywhere. Whilst the Lord's Prayer reflects a very personal relationship, it has in its view the very grandest horizons.

A shocking privilege

Our Father is *in heaven*. This is a reminder of the greatness of our God; that he dwells in unapproachable light, and so it is a shocking privilege to be able to come to the throne of grace at will and be heard.

Heaven is the throne room of the Lord God Almighty (Isaiah 66:1). From there, the Lord of all is able to answer our prayers, no matter how impossible they may seem (Ephesians 3:20-21). That our Father is in heaven is good news.

But heaven also functions in a second way in the Sermon on the Mount. The kingdom of heaven is our inheritance, if we are persecuted for righteousness. Our reward is in heaven. And with superior righteousness, we can expect to enter the kingdom of heaven (Matthew 5:10-20). So it is throughout the Sermon. If it is about relating well to our heavenly Father whilst here on earth, it is also about keeping our eyes on our final destination.

We pray "our Father in heaven" both because that is where he is, and because it is where we are heading.

Our highest regard

The prayer then turns from addressing God to our first petition, or request. Here Jesus sets the agenda, the priorities, for all prayer. We are to pray "hallowed be your name". In the Bible, the name stands in for the whole person, so that the way a name is honoured, to that extent the person is honoured.

Jesus teaches us that the highest priority of our prayers ought to be the honouring of God's name. Of course, we don't tend to use the word "hallowed" much these days. It is probably familiar to most of us only from this prayer, or from Harry Potter! But for all that, we are probably familiar with the idea. To hallow means to hold in the highest regard.

It should not surprise us that God's honour is to be our first and highest regard. It is, after all, *God's* highest regard. Ephesians 1 repeatedly tells us that God acts for the praise of his glory and his grace (Ephesians 1:6, 12, 14). God tells Israel that he acts primarily for his name's sake (Ezekiel 36:22). God is concerned that people see him for who he really is. That governs world history. It ought to govern our prayers.

Jesus does not limit the prayer in any way. We are to pray that God is honoured in our words and in our lives. But way more than that, he is to be honoured in the world. The triumph of God's name throughout the world is to be our prayer.

He is our Father in heaven, and he cares for us. But he is our Father, and we must care for his honour too.

Questions for Reflection

1. How does God being your Father encourage you to pray?

2. How does God being our Father in heaven challenge your prayers?

3. How does Jesus's priority for the honour of God challenge your prayers?

Prayer

Our Father in heaven,
thank you that, through Jesus, you are are indeed our Father.
Thank you for drawing me into your family.
Please bring glory to yourself in me,
in my family, in my church, and in the world,
through our thoughts, our words and deeds.
In Jesus's name,
Amen.

A Dangerous Prayer

"Your kingdom come."

Matthew 6:10, Luke 11:2

In Matthew 6:33, Jesus goes on to command us to "seek first his kingdom." As we have seen, the whole Sermon on the Mount is intended to teach us what being kingdom people means. So it should come as little surprise to us that Jesus, having rightly begun with the hallowing of God himself, should then turn his attention to what God is primarily doing in the world. He is bringing his kingdom.

A Kingdom needs a King

The word "kingdom" is meaningless if there is no king. There are plenty of alternative political systems, and Jesus could have talked about God's rule as a democracy if he had wanted to do so. But God is interested in establishing an absolute monarchy. Indeed, establishing his King in Zion is an act of aggression (Psalm 2:7). He places his King on his throne *against* the nations who conspire to break off God's chains, to dismiss his rule (Psalm 2:1-3). In other words, the coming of the kingdom is going to, finally, bring an end to all rebellion, all sin.

At the same time, the King is the one through whom God has promised to fulfil all of his promises. When great King David's greater Son arrived, he would establish a kingdom of blessing and glory forever (2 Samuel 7).

Where is the kingdom?

We might well ask where, then, is the kingdom. After all, Jesus has come as the King but the nations of the earth still stand in opposition to Christ. This should not alarm us. Jesus declared that, "My kingdom is not of this world" (John 18:36). Jesus came the first time, not to establish a political nation within this world, but to save a people from it for the kingdom that is to come.

In other words, the fullness of the kingdom, its greatest expression, is still future, when the New Heavens and the New Earth come down out of heaven from God (Revelation 21:2). We might call that the glorified kingdom, where it is seen in all its true beauty.

But the kingdom is not absent today. The kingdom of Jesus is found wherever the King is acknowledged. Wherever God turns human hearts—from creaturely loves for money, sex, power, fame, or any combination of these and other idols, towards the only true King—there is the kingdom found. This is not necessarily obvious to see. Two people may walk down the street side by side, one belonging to the kingdom of this world in rebellion against God, and the other in Jesus's kingdom. We are not in the glorified kingdom yet.

Rather, wherever we find Christians, there is the kingdom of grace. It is the community of believers, the Church. It is the place where Christ rules by his Word.

What are we really praying?

When we pray those three little words, "Your kingdom come", we are praying very great things. We are praying for extraordinary miracles.

To begin with, we are praying for *conversions*. We are praying that God would overrule in the hearts of rebels so that they would have a new heart, a new spirit, a new principle of life (Ezekiel 36:26-27). A new rule. That they would turn from their rebellion and come under the rule of Christ. It is the prayer that we should pray for our family, friends, neighbours and, indeed, enemies.

More than that, we are praying for *global conversions*. Jesus sent the Church, after all, to make disciples of all nations because Jesus is the King of all kings and the Lord of the nations (Matthew 28:18-19). It is the prayer that we should pray for our church's mission partners, and for those parts of the world where the gospel is least known, as well as for our local mission.

Secondly, it is a prayer for *the return of Christ*. It is the prayer of John in Revelation 22:20, at the very end of the Bible, when Jesus tells John that he is coming soon. John replies, "Come, Lord Jesus." The full expression of the Kingdom of Jesus, the suppression of all enmity, and the glorification of his people will not happen until Jesus returns. To pray for his kingdom to come is to pray for the end of this world.

It is a prayer according to God's priorities. It is a prayer for the extension of the church to every part of every community around the world, as we wait with eager expectation for the final coming of the Kingdom. It is a prayer that therefore also implies our intention. To be kingdom people, under the rule of Christ, and to have his priorities, and to pray for their flourishing, is also to offer ourselves in his service. It is a dangerous prayer. To pray "Your kingdom come" is to be willing to go. It is to ask Jesus to extend his rule in the world as we offer ourselves as those who will take that saving gospel to our part of the world. Perhaps even to the furthest reaches of the world.

If we pray this seriously, we can expect God to do extraordinary things. He might even choose to do them through us.

Questions for Reflection

1. What expectations do you have about how God could answer this prayer?

2. What might it mean for you to be willing to be used by God to fulfil this prayer?

3. Think of ways you can pray for God's kingdom to come around the whole world.

Prayer

Our Father in Heaven,
You have established King Jesus in the New Zion,
but his rule is contested here on Earth,
and many millions languish for lack of a Saviour.
Please bring your Kingdom in all its fullness.
We long for the end of all rebellion,
so turn hearts to Christ in every corner of the world,
that your kingdom may be made of those from every tribe,
       tongue, and nation.
And, heavenly Father,
I offer you my services, such as they are,
that you might bless them in extending Christ's rule.
In his name, and for your glory,
Amen.

A Submissive Prayer

"Your will be done, on earth as in heaven."

Matt 6:10

At first glance, praying "Your will be done" seems to be somewhat self-contradictory. Some reading this will believe that God is absolutely sovereign, in charge, in which case *everything* that happens is God's will. God's will is *always* done, and that won't be changed by prayer. On the other hand, some of us will struggle to believe that God is really sovereign at all. In which case, the prayer is more like telling God that we *hope* his will is done, rather than asking him to *make* it so. In either case, the prayer can strike us as a little odd.

Jesus himself prays as though God is sovereign and in control. In Matthew 26:39, he is in the garden at Gethsemane, and he submits his will to the will of the Father with these words: "My Father, if it is possible, may this cup be taken from me. Yet not as I will, but as you will."

Jesus submits his future to the plan of God. But he does so knowing that God is willing and able to bring his plans to pass. Indeed, he acknowledges that his will is impossible if it is against God's will. The Father's plan to save a people through the cross will not be undone by Caiaphas or Pilate just because they don't want to play their parts. Jesus submits to the sovereign plan of God.

Some of us will struggle with this idea, because it sounds as though God does everything, including evil things, so it is worth a comment on this in passing. There are a variety of occasions where the Bible speaks of *one* action with *two* intentions. A great example of this is the story of Joseph, sold by his brothers into slavery, then wrongly imprisoned. Mistreated for years before being raised to a position where he could deliver God's people from famine. In Genesis 50:20, Joseph shows his prophetic gift when he says, "You intended to harm me, but God intended it for good to accomplish what is now being done, the saving of many lives." The same event, Joseph being sold into slavery, was intended to do great harm by his brothers, but God was doing something different. He was saving thousands of lives, including the critical line of promise, through Joseph's pain. We pray to a sovereign God.

To bring about God's purpose

God's will is always done, through the good and bad times. So why pray this prayer?

There are two answers to this question. The first is that, frequently, biblical prayers are on the basis of the things God has revealed about himself and his plan. So when Moses intercedes for the people of Israel after they commit idolatry with the golden calf, Moses appeals to God's reputation. God has spent much of the book up to that point declaring that he will act for his name's sake, so that the people will know who he is (e.g. Exodus 6:7). So Moses appeals to God not to destroy the people *because it will reflect badly on him* (Exodus 32:12). Moses knows that God is acting for his greater glory, and destroying the Israelites will in some sense diminish that glory. Moses prays, in other words, according to what God has already promised to do. And God works *through those prayers* to bring about his purpose.

So we should pray for the things that God has promised to do because our prayers are part of God's means of fulfilling his purposes.

God's will for us

But there is a second sense of God's will. If the first is about what God is doing directly, this second is about what God has revealed to us as his will for us. It is the sum of all the directions the Bible gives to us. It is living according to his wisdom. It is living in the fear of the Lord.

When we pray, "Your will be done", we are praying that God would help us and all his people to obey him. To make us more like Jesus. That is the context of this entire prayer, as Jesus spends the Sermon on the Mount teaching his people how to live as Kingdom people. They are to be perfect, just like him (Matthew 5:48).

Indeed, the whole Gospel tends in this direction. Jesus ends it, after all, commanding the church to make disciples of all nations. Not converts only, but disciples. And disciples, "obey everything I have commanded you" (Matthew 28:20).

The standard here is very high. It is to be in perfect submission to Christ, here on earth just as his court is in heaven. Again, this is a dangerous prayer. If the previous line is about God broadening the church, this is a prayer for him to deepen it. To aim at perfect maturity. For us. For our church. For every church. It is the prayer that invites God to go to war against our own sin.

This is a prayer of personal submission to Christ. It is going to be costly. It doesn't come naturally to us to submit to Christ; everything in our flesh wants to rebel. This is why Paul characterises this manner of life as putting to death whatever belongs to our old nature (Colossians 3:5). This is not the easy path. It is not fun. It is to take the narrow, difficult way. Just as it was in the garden, when Jesus submitted his desire to avoid pain to the Father's will to save an unnumbered multitude. When we pray this prayer, we are walking in the footsteps of our King.

How will God answer this prayer?

This is a prayer for maturity. Growing to be like Jesus is becoming more fully human, restored to what we were intended to be. But how do we get there? How can we expect God to answer this prayer?

Paul gives us great clarity on this point. He tells us that we grow to maturity *together* as we speak the truth in love to one another (Ephesians 4:15). Is this *any* truth though? Is it enough to speak the truth about the weather, or the sport? No! But there is one truth that is sufficient by itself to make any person mature. It is the truth about Jesus (Ephesians 4:21). In every situation, to Jew or Gentile, old or young, male or female, slave or free, Paul simply preaches the fullness of the truth that is in Jesus, and people grow in maturity (Colossians 1:28).

Elsewhere he tells us that as the truth about Jesus is laid before us, as we take time to dwell upon it, we are contemplating the face of the Saviour. As we dwell on him, as we grow to love him more, as our hearts are turned to love the things he loves and hate the things he hates, as we see how he responds to this world, and we seek to imitate him, so we grow "from one degree of glory to another" (2 Corinthians 3:18).

So what shall we do? "Set our hearts and minds on things above, where Christ is" (Colossians 3:1-4). When we pray, "Your will be done", we are committing to a life spent contemplating Christ, so that he will grow our obedience.

Questions for Reflection

1. Why do we need to be willing for God to change us when we pray this prayer?

2. What are the areas in your own life into which you know you need to pray this prayer?

3. How can you "set your heart and mind on things above" more effectively?

Prayer

Our Father in heaven,
you know that every fibre of my sinful self
longs to rebel against my Saviour.
But you will finish the good work you have started in me.
So, Lord, I pray that you will subdue my flesh,
give me victory over my sinful nature,
and give me such a sweet contemplation of Christ,
that I love him above all else,
that I may love what he loves and hate what he hates.
In Jesus's name,
Amen.

A Daily Prayer

"Give us today our daily bread."

Matt 6:11, Luke 11:3

Here, halfway through the prayer, we turn from our concerns for God's honour and his purposes in our lives, to what we might call our concerns about our lives. Of course, this distinction is false, for in praying for God's will to be done, we have prayed very much for ourselves. Nevertheless, this is at least a turn to pray for the things that we all need, whether Christian or not.

A daily prayer

It is worth pausing to reflect that Jesus seems to expect this to be our *daily* prayer. We are, after all, praying today for our daily bread, not for next week or next month. Tomorrow will be a new day when this prayer will be needed again. In that sense, this is perhaps a prayer for first thing in the morning, committing the needs of the day into God's hands.

A challenging prayer

This is a deeply challenging prayer for a number of reasons.

First, it reminds us of our *total dependence* on God for every good thing we have. In saying "Give", we are not usually asking God to send manna from heaven, as though he does not use ordinary means to give us what we need. Rather, it recognises the fact that our jobs, for example, are his means of providing for our needs. They are as much a gift of his grace, as manna was for the Israelites.

Of course, it may be the case that we really are in dire financial need, and very aware of our dependence on God. In which case, we will need no further encouragement to pray, simply to remember that God is our generous Father who delights to answer our prayers.

Secondly, this prayer challenges us to *pray for those things that many of us take for granted*. We so rarely pray for our daily needs because we think that we can provide them. We are very happy to pray for things that are well beyond our reach, but for our daily needs, often less so.

This, in turn, kills our thanksgiving. How often do we get to the end of the day and think about how we've seen God's sustaining grace in a whole variety of ways? How little joy we experience in the Christian life because we do not notice his daily provisions!

Thirdly, *this prayer attacks our idols*. Where we might pray for some extraordinary blessing, Jesus seems to think that it is quite sufficient to pray for our needs. If we have shelter, food, and clothing, basic necessities, should we not be thankful for that? Should we not be content?

By praying this prayer, we are asking God not to satisfy our idolatrous love for other things. This is completely in line with the tenth commandment against covetousness. It is our natural condition to look to the future and desire many things which may not be God's good plan for us. Here we place ourselves into God's hands, committing to do our daily jobs, and trusting that he will provide everything he decides that we need. It is a prayer that rests both on his generosity and his wisdom for the day ahead.

Bread here is the main staple food. It isn't olive oil or meat, which would have been luxuries, but basic needs for the richest to the poorest. How much we take for granted the kindnesses of God until such things are taken away!

This is a remarkable contrast to consumerist Western society. Jesus's prayer here challenges us to be content, thankful even, for the simple necessities we have, and to bless others with our excess. Similarly, Paul tells the thief in Ephesus to stop stealing, taking daily provisions from others, but instead work in order to be able to share with others (Ephesians 4:28).

Perhaps this is even Christ's way of gently waking us up to the distressing reality that there are people in our midst who know the daily fear of running out of food, and who cry out to the Lord for his provision. As we pray "Give us today our daily bread", will we be God's means of answering that prayer for others in our congregations, for those in our communities who are suffering, for those in other churches in less privileged situations, and even for other believers around the world?

Let us not only pray the prayer. Let us also be God's means of graciously answering it for others.

Questions for Reflection

1. What is it that you wish God would provide for you? What do you *need* him to provide for you?

2. Why don't you make a list of everything that God has provided for you today?

3. How might this prayer make you more generous with what God has given you?

Prayer

Our Father in Heaven,
grant us eyes to see your great grace in our daily provision.
Help us to see our great need
for you to give us life and breath, bread and shelter.
Give us the humility to rejoice each day
in the mercies you have poured out.
Cause us to dwell on your generosity,
and to be a channel of your grace towards others,
for your glory, in Jesus's name,
Amen.

A Glorious Prayer

"Forgive us our sins, as we forgive those who sin against us."

Matt 6:12, Luke 11:4

Given how short the Lord's Prayer is, and how very many great needs there are in the world, it would no doubt puzzle a worldly person that we are taught to pray about our sins. But a moment's reflection will show us that so much of the misery in the world is rooted in sin. Sometimes this is a matter of direct cause and effect as when, for example, an affair leads to broken marriages. But just as prevalent are the consequences of living in a world groaning under the curse of God (Romans 8:20). The brokenness of the world, in every respect, is a result of Adam's first sin: crime and natural disasters, disease and death. Sin is *the* great problem in the world.

And it is the great problem for us *personally*. As our study of the ten commandments has shown, our hearts naturally turn to serve ourselves, and we lie, and lust, and steal, and certainly we covet. The effects of our sin on those around us, and the consequent effect on our lives, is terrifying.

Once we have grasped something of the scale of the "sin problem" we can begin to stagger in wonder at what Jesus does here. He commands us to pray, "Forgive us!" He invites us to expect God to forgive us.

Now, of course, we might be tempted to think that forgiving is what God does, like a benevolent uncle when you knock over his tea. If we think like this, then we will not grasp the glory of what Jesus is saying here.

In Matthew 18, Jesus tells the parable of the unmerciful servant. There is a King, who in the parable stands in for God, who calls in his debts. A servant comes before him who owes him ten thousand talents. Now, that already sounds like a lot, but it doesn't really capture our imagination. The footnote in my Bible tells me that a talent was about 20 years' wages for a day labourer. In new money, that is maybe £500,000. And this servant owes *ten thousand of those*! Here is a man who owes his king £5 billion.

That is our state before God. Hopelessly in debt, and with no means of paying the debt. We are ruined, and the servant knows it. He cries out for mercy because that is all he can do.

That is our spiritual state before God. Our sin corrupts everything we are and do, and the degree of our failure to reach God's standards is breathtaking. Just consider what has come before in the prayer: Do we hallow God's name? Do we do on earth what is done in heaven? Seek first the Kingdom? Give thanks for all his daily provision? Hardly at all.

So all we can do is rely on the mercy of God. And Jesus teaches us to expect God to forgive us.

As we forgive those who sin against us

But this glorious prayer has a sting in the tail. To be forgiven people, to have our great debt before God cancelled through Christ's death in our place, means that we must stand in a new relationship to others. Knowing the value of forgiveness, and how great our debt was, we should be willing to cancel the debt of others.

Indeed, the point is rather sharper: Jesus frames the prayer so that we actually ask God to apply to *our* forgiveness the degree of mercy that we ourselves use with *others*. It is a dangerous prayer, because it makes our forgiveness conditional on our forgiving others.

In this prayer, we ask God to *only* forgive us in the way that we forgive others. So if we hold the debts of others against them then we should expect God to do the same with us.

Jesus illustrates this in the parable of the unmerciful servant. Having had his £5bn debt cancelled, the servant goes out to find another servant. This servant owes him a considerable sum, about £20,000. I think it is deliberate that the debt is so large. In any ordinary situation we would expect him to pursue this debt. But, having received so much clemency, so that he doesn't need to find £5bn, surely he can forgive others such a relatively small amount?

Perhaps we need to pause before we pray this prayer again. We should ask whether we *really* want God to apply this to us? If in our hearts we refuse to forgive others, if the gall of bitterness has taken root and flourishes in our relationships, then this is a most dangerous prayer to pray.

That is not in any way to diminish the great harm that may have been done to us. Perhaps we had an abusive parent, a cheating spouse, a child who robbed us or any number of other, truly horrible, things done to us. I don't think Jesus is dismissing these as small things. And God himself will be their judge, far better than we can. But whatever has been done to us, we need to see that we have done far worse to God. We have have lived our whole lives for ourselves, neglected him and his gifts, spoiled his world by our self-centredness.

In other words, this is a prayer that can only *safely* be prayed by one who has truly grasped the scale of their sin against God. Only by seeing the harm done by others in its proper comparison to the harm we have done to God, can we forgive others and so receive full pardon from God. Of course, we will struggle to do this perfectly, and I don't think Jesus is making our perfect forgiveness contingent on perfectly forgiving others. But the spirit has to be right.

In the parable, the king calls the servant back in and says to him, 'Shouldn't you have had mercy on your fellow servant just as I had on you?' Then, he removes his forgiveness from this man and places him in prison. Of course, this is an incomplete account of what happens when we are wronged and we haven't space here to think about the need for repentance by those who have done wrong. But it would be wise for us to take seriously Jesus's teaching, and to consider whether there are any people for whom we harbour bitterness, and an unforgiving spirit. If we do, we need to realise that it is ourselves most of all who are endangered by it.

Questions for Reflection

1. How does knowledge that you are forgiven by God help you to forgive other people?

2. Who do you struggle to forgive? Why?

3. Are there any active steps towards forgiving others that you need to take today?

Prayer

Our Father in Heaven,
give me grace to forgive others as you have first forgiven me.
Help me to see the wonder and scale of your mercy to me,
so that I may extend the same mercy to others.
Lord, some people have hurt me,
and I have held on to that bitterness too long.
Help me by your Spirit to be at peace with all people,
trusting that you will bring your justice in the end.
In Jesus's name, Amen.

A Transforming Prayer

"Lead us not into temptation."

Matt 6:13, Luke 11:4

We are in a battle

In the previous chapter, we recalled the very great debt that we owe to God for our sin, which needs to be forgiven because we have no means of paying it ourselves. Today, we turn from our past failures to the day which lies ahead of us, and we cry out to God to be kept from being overwhelmed by temptation to sin.

The world is full of distraction and attraction. Our hearts long for the New Creation but, because we cannot see the joy that will be ours on that final day, we are tempted to satisfy that longing in all manner of ways now. We seek happiness in relationships, in our professional reputation, in being well regarded by others for good works, in making money. Perhaps more likely, we look to some combination of all of these, and more besides. As John Calvin said, our hearts are factories of idols.

Ephesians 6:11-12 reminds us that our temptations are a tool of the devil, and our battle *for* the unseen New Creation with Christ is *against* the unseen demonic powers who play on our longings. The world is full of good things which the flesh and the devil make out to be ultimately important things.

We are not alone

Wonderfully, we are not alone. "Because he himself suffered when he was tempted, he is able to help those who are being tempted" (Hebrews 2:18). Christ has shared in our humanity and has faced all the same temptations we do, and yet was without sin. Our longings are not sin, though the way we seek to satisfy them can be. Moreover, Jesus knows how hard it is to remain sinless. In Hebrews his experience is called *suffering*. It is more painful to resist sin than it is to give in; and Jesus never gave in. The battle was most fierce in the life of Christ.

For example, Christ was tempted at the beginning of his earthly ministry, in the wilderness. Just before the Lord's Prayer (Matthew 4, Luke 4), we are told that Jesus spent forty days in the wilderness without food. I imagine that he was desperately hungry, and the devil tempts Jesus to turn rocks, of which there were plenty, into bread. He tempts him to prove God's love for him. He tempts him to take dominion of the world without the cross. These must have been great temptations. But all three times Jesus resists the devil with the word of God.

We also see the suffering of Christ in resisting the devil and submitting to God in the Garden of Gethsemane. Already Christ knows what is before him, the pain that will be his on the cross. He was in such anguish that he sweated blood. Yet he was determined that he would not rebel, would not allow his temptation to run away overcome the plan of God for our redemption.

Oh yes, Christ knows very well the struggle with sin.

Not a withdrawal from the world

We might be tempted to think that the safest approach is to withdraw from the world. After all, if we lived on a remote island, away from people, there would be a lot fewer temptations! There is a long tradition of monastic withdrawal from the world, but that was not the path that Jesus chose. He deliberately came *into* the world from a place of perfect contentment where the devil could not touch him, in order to secure the redemption of the world. We are not called to be monks and nuns, or hermits living in a cave. We are to be his ambassadors, proclaiming his victory, in the world.

Moreover, we need to be careful that we don't fall into less-than-Christian ideas about the world. The world itself is not evil. The ancient Greeks were often very negative about the material world, and that has bled over into some Christians' thinking about, for example, sex and marriage, which is why Roman Catholic priests are forbidden to marry. Once we recognise that good things can be corrupted (and they really are in our materialistic Western culture at the moment), we will be tempted (and I use that word deliberately) to consider the good things God made to be bad things.

No! God made the world and he made it very good. He filled it with beauty and wonder, and pours out his abundant blessings in his common and saving graces, day by day. We must not neglect or ignore these good things that God has given to us.

Avoiding temptation is not about avoiding the world. Of course, sometimes there are things that tempt us which it is wise for us to avoid. An alcoholic should probably avoid the pubs and bars, for instance. But even then, his temptations do not make pubs and bars inherently evil. "Do not be mislead: 'Bad company corrupts good character'" (1 Corinthians 15:33).

To love the world, without being in love with it

Rather, we have been called to be in the world, but not of it. We are to love the world, pouring ourselves out in loving service and gospel proclamation, without being *in love* with it. In other words, what we are praying here is that we will see the world as it really is. To see it as God sees it. To feel about it the way God feels about it.

We are praying that we can encounter everything that God has made with the same spirit, the same attitude, the same love as Christ did, who walked this earth without sin. How do we do that? Paul tells us in Galatians 6:14 that we must consider the world crucified to us, and ourselves to the world. We are to kill our love for worldly things that in any way oppose, or distract from, Christ.

We cannot drive out false loves without replacing them with true and better loves. If we are to put down our temptations, we must learn to regard the things that tempt us in the right way, because we love God more. Far more. And so we need to come back to Christ: who he is, what he has done, is doing and, gloriously, will do for us on the final day. We must set our hearts and minds above, where Christ is, seated at the right hand of the Father (Colossians 3:1-4) so that our love for earthly things grows dim by comparison.

This is not a prayer for God to keep us from the things we often find tempting, as wise as it may be for us to avoid certain temptations. Rather, it is a prayer that we would no longer find tempting the things that used to captivate us because we are consumed with a greater love: Christ.

Questions for Reflection

1. What are the things that you tend to love more than you should?

2. Are there places it would be wise for you not to go, or people it would be wise for you not to see?

3. What can you do to ensure that you set your heart and mind on Christ and heaven today?

Prayer

Our Father in heaven,
Give me grace today to love you above all things,
through Jesus Christ, my glorious Saviour and Lord.
Make dull to me the things of this world that once tempted me.
Cause my love for them to diminish as my love for you grows,
so that I may pass through this world, enjoying the beauty of it,
without being corrupted by temptation.
Keep me safe from the deceptiveness of sin.
In Jesus's name,
Amen.

A Victorious Prayer

"But deliver us from evil."
Matthew 6:13

The concept of evil is a prominent one in Jesus's teaching in Matthew's Gospel. It is worth getting our bearings on it because it is so easy for us to forget that evil is real, Satan is real, and our fight in this life is against the spiritual powers that oppose us (Ephesians 6:12).

The evil one

In the parable of the sower, Jesus talks about the *evil one*, which is Satan (13:19). That is a shocking thing; that any being is characterised by evil to the extent that he can be called '*the* Evil One' is alarming. In the parable, the evil one is snatching the word of the gospel from the hearts of those who are thereby prevented from believing the gospel. If this prayer leads us to anything, it should surely be to pray against this ministry of the devil.

Not only is he opposed to the truth, but he is a *liar* (John 8:44). He deceives by masquerading as an angel of light (2 Corinthians 11:14) in order to lead believers and unbelievers alike away from God's word and his ways. Moreover, when he manages to deceive, then he becomes the *accuser* (Revelation 12:10), bringing before the throne of God the great list of our sins which, but for the blood of Christ, would exclude us from the throne of grace. So he is evil in relation to our spiritual life and death.

But the evil one is not restricted to spiritual attack. Job speaks of the events that happened to him as being "evil" (Job 30:26). The evil is not from God (Job 34:10) who works in all things for our good (Romans 8:28). They are from the devil's desire to destroy him. Satan desires Job to curse God (Job 1:11). There is an evil one, who has evil schemes to trap us and turn us from God, and there are evil events from the hands of the devil, that are intended to cause us to curse God.

We are to pray for deliverance from the evil one. And we are to pray that God would deliver us from evil in the world.

Evil in us

But it is here that Jesus is, perhaps, even more shocking. To begin with, Jesus diagnoses the great sin problem as evil in our hearts (Matthew 15:19). Similarly, he says to the very people to whom he is teaching this prayer, "If you, then, *who are evil*, know how to give good gifts to your children, how much more will your Father in heaven give good gifts to those who ask him" (Matthew 7:11). Compared to God, the only true definition of goodness, we are evil and we need to pray for God to deliver us from the worst inclinations of our sinful nature which lives on.

Of course, if there is evil in the hearts of believers, how much more in those Jesus calls "sons of the evil one" (Matthew 13:38). All people in the world have a spiritual parent. Jesus has encouraged us to call God our Father, and to bear his family likeness. Although sin persists in us, it doesn't characterise us as it once did, and as it does those whose father is the evil one. They are incapable of pleasing God (Romans 8:8). Of course, that doesn't mean that anyone is as evil as they might be. But it does mean that the devil has deceitfully led them away from Christ in order to do his work.

That work sometimes means falsely accusing Christians (Matthew 5:11). It will ultimately mean bringing out of their hearts the wicked things stored there (Matthew 12:35).

Evil in the curse

In all this, we need to remember that the world is under the curse of God from Genesis 3. Suffering, sickness, and death are an expression of God's anger at our evil hearts, at our sinful rebellion. The presence of evil spirits around the ministry of Jesus is of a piece with this.

But the key thing for us to remember is this: Jesus has triumphed over all evil spirits, including the devil himself, in his life, death, resurrection, and ascension.

Focus on the Deliverer

The temptation for us is to stop there. To recognise that there are a variety of evils in the world, and all have something of the character of *the* evil one.

But the point of the prayer is that there is one who is greater than the evil one. We turn to prayer because we are incapable of standing firm by ourselves. We could not cure our hearts. We were spiritually dead like everyone else (Ephesians 2:1-3).

The glory of the gospel is that Jesus came into the world to prove God's victory over every one of these evils. The devil may accuse us, but it is God who justifies us (Romans 8:33).

Jesus speaks of a strong man who is overpowered, bound, and has his house plundered (Matthew 12:29). The devil is the strong man. Too strong for you and me. But Jesus came into a world controlled by the devil and bound him. He robbed him of any power at the cross, and plundered his kingdom of billions of unbelievers who then turned to Christ. Every conversion is a victory over a powerless enemy.

As Christ cast out demons, opened the eyes of the blind, and even raised the dead, he rolled back the curse and proved that he alone has sovereign power. And one day all that is evil in the world will be refined in the fire, and the purified people of God will be restored to his eternal kingdom, as the devil and all his minions are cast into the outer darkness (Revelation 20:10).

When we pray for God to deliver us from evil, we do it as people who have already been delivered from the devil's accusations and from his control. One day we know we will be delivered from the presence of evil altogether.

So we cry out in prayer to a God who has proven himself willing and able. Like any good Father, he will protect us if we will call to him.

Questions for Reflection

1. What difference does it make to know that God is your Father who loves you and will deliver you from evil?

2. How does it help to remember that God has *already* delivered you from the curse of the Fall (Genesis 3)?

3. Why do we need to keep praying this prayer?

Prayer

Our Father in Heaven,
thank you for Jesus.
Thank you that he has already dealt with my evil,
        my guilt and shame.
Thank you that one day you will deliver me from the presence
        of all evil and into your perfect heavenly kingdom.
Please deliver me today from all the ministry of the devil.
Help me by your Spirit to keep trusting Jesus most of all.
In his name,
Amen.

A Prayer of Celebration

"For the kingdom, the power and the glory are yours,
now and forever, Amen."

Matthew 6:13 (some manuscripts)

This final line doesn't appear in Luke's shorter account of the prayer, nor in the early manuscripts of Matthew's account. Whether these are a direct quotation from Jesus is hard to substantiate, but we retain them in the Anglican liturgy because they express glorious truths that we would do well to take to heart.

All is the Father's

We turn at this point from asking God to do something for his own name, or for our personal preservation, and instead recognise things that are. We are not so much asking God to do something in the future, as pointing out what he has already done through Christ. It is the part of the prayer in which we are most inclined to simply say, "Wow!"

The prayer turns back from us to God: these things "are yours." As we shall see below, we are wrapped up in this prayer; we belong to the Father. But the prayer ends where it began, focused squarely on God and his possession of us, rather than where many of our prayers start and end, with ourselves.

Forever

Let's just notice the scope of the prayer as well, before we look at the content of it. We have said that the kingdom, the power, and the glory are God's now. This is the state of play. But it is also a state that will run, uninterrupted, for the rest of eternity. This final part of the prayer acknowledges no alternatives, and brooks no rivals. All that is God's now will never be taken from him. As Jesus tells us, the Father has given the church into Christ's hands, and nobody is strong enough to take us from him (John 10:28).

The Kingdom

The definite article is important here: it is *the* kingdom. There is only one kingdom that matters. It is the one established when the Father installed his King in Zion (Psalm 2:7). Where the eternal king is, there is the eternal kingdom of God, which Jesus will bring to its full consummation and then hand back to the Father. In that sense, the kingdom is the work of Jesus.

As we remember that Christ died for the church, and that only those bought with the blood of Christ may ever enter into the kingdom, we remember that the kingdom is not an abstract thing. It is a precious and dearly loved people. It is Christ's kingdom.

It is us. When we pray "the kingdom … is yours", we are, above all things, saying "*We* are yours." Even as the prayer ends focused on God, we are committing ourselves to him, and to the rule of his king.

In other words, this is not simply an observation of a wonderful fact, but a celebration that God holds us in his hands, as his precious and dearly loved children and that, more than anything, he is the centre not only of our prayers but our lives as well.

The Power

It is tempting to look at the pain and suffering in the world and become almost dualistic. That is, to think that God is *a* power, but that the devil is an equal power, each winning some battles, losing others. If we thought like that, we would live in constant fear that, for all his promises, and his supposed sovereignty, there is no certainty of anything in the future, because God is not *really* in control at all.

But again, we here recognise only one power, *the* power, and it is all God's. Whether kings, parliaments, military commanders, your boss, your pastor, you parents—every power in the universe only exists because God made it, and upholds it by the power of his will. All power in the universe is entirely derived from what God chooses to permit. The devil is on a leash, only able to do what God allows him to do in the fulfilment of God's greater plan.

Both we and anyone who opposes us are under the sovereign hand of God. Should we be afraid of an increasingly secular culture? There is only one kingdom that matters, and there is only one power that matters. Our opponents may hate Christ and his gospel, but they will fulfil the hidden will of God by opposing him. It is often in the face of opposition that the church has most flourished. In the words of the early church writer Tertullian, "The blood of the martyrs is the seed of the Church."

Indeed, the power of God is deliberately focused on *building* the church (Ephesians 2:19-22) even as the devil seeks to tear us apart (Ephesians 6:10-13). Christ will build his church. He has disarmed the powers that stood against us, triumphing over them at the cross (Colossians 2:15).

All of which means, that praying "the power… is yours" is a wonderful statement of our security. It is a wonderful statement that the plan of God, and the consummation of the New Creation are utterly secure. These words are a celebration.

The Glory

God is seen to be glorious when he is seen as he truly is. God is glorious. Yet to so many in our world, he is a figure of fun, a useful swear word, and nothing more.

To the church, however, we confess his glory. We may see as through a glass darkly; we do not have the privilege of seeing the transfiguration with our earthly eyes. Yet we get to gaze on the glory of God in the face of Christ (2 Corinthians 4:6). As we see all of Christ in all the Scriptures, as we dwell on his beauty in all its facets, so we see his glory. And so we see the character of the Father manifest in the person and work of Jesus. There we see the glory of God, the glory that he has now, and which will be fully revealed at the coming of Christ.

How do we respond to this? Surely as John the Baptist did, by saying "He must increase and I must decrease" (John 3:30).

Insofar as we manage to grasp the reality that the only kingdom, all the power, and the infinite glory are the Father's, to that extent we will find contentment in being in the kingdom, under his plan and power, and heading for the certainty of his eternal home.

And so we say, "Amen."

Questions for Reflection

1. What does it mean for Christ to be your King?

2. As you face the day before you, what difference does it make to do it in God's strength?

3. Where do you look to see the glory of God manifest now?

Prayer

Our Father in Heaven,
it is my privilege to be part of your kingdom,
under the loving rule of King Jesus.
Please help me to live in obedience to my king today.
It is also my great joy to live under your mighty protective hand,
    my loving Father.
Help me to trust that all the power is yours, and will be forever,
and nobody can take me from your hand.
Finally, please help me to see your glory,
and reflect it in my life,
so that you are glorified in me and in your church,
now and forever.
Amen.

The church and the sacraments

Baptism

Lee Gatiss

"Then the eleven disciples went to Galilee, to the mountain where Jesus had told them to go. When they saw him, they worshipped him; but some doubted. Then Jesus came to them and said, 'All authority in heaven and on earth has been given to me. Therefore go and make disciples of all nations, baptising them in the name of the Father and of the Son and of the Holy Spirit, and teaching them to obey everything I have commanded you. And surely I am with you always, to the very end of the age.'"
Matthew 28:16-20

In the next three chapters we are going to think in a bit more detail about baptism, the Lord's Supper, and the church. Christians normally meet up every week for church, and we regularly have baptisms and celebrate the supper. But we don't always think very carefully (or at all) about why we do these things! So it is worth us giving them some attention here.

We start with baptism. Often we don't appreciate what baptism is really all about. There's been confusion about what it means and what it doesn't mean, and Christians can disagree with each other about it. Sometimes that means we avoid talking about it. And so either we forget about it altogether or we downplay its significance or don't bother to think straight about it. But since baptism is so important in the Bible, it is important for us as Christians to be clear on it.

In many churches there are a variety of views on what baptism is and who is qualified to receive it. We tolerate that variety because we think of those disagreements as disagreements over secondary issues. The Roman Catholic church does not think of baptism as a secondary issue though. To put it at its most blunt: if one is not baptised then one is not saved, in Roman Catholic teaching. But Protestants don't follow that line. Baptism is not absolutely essential for salvation (though it is a normal part of the Christian life). So it is a secondary issue.

On the other hand, just because we can disagree on it and not imperil our salvation as a result, does not suddenly make baptism unimportant. That's a great mistake. Secondary issues are massively important, and it is vital we get our heads straight about them. Even if it means we don't break fellowship with one another because of them.

So it's crucial that we examine what the Bible says about baptism. We might have all sorts of disagreements over some aspects of this—and I will try to point out where those disagreements usually arise. But that shouldn't make us go silent or stop thinking about the subject. It should just make us more than usually careful. After all, it is important for us, as Christians, to learn to disagree on secondary issues without having a punch up.

Inward spiritual gifts

There's a standard theological definition of baptism which goes like this: baptism is an outward and physical sign of an inward and spiritual grace. Another way to put it is that baptism is a visible picture of an invisible present.

So there are two parts to baptism. On the one hand—the outward sign, the visible picture; on the other hand—the inward spiritual gift, the invisible present. Let's look at those two aspects of baptism, in reverse order.

So first, what are the inward spiritual gifts or invisible presents from God that lie behind baptism? What is it *really* all about? To use biblical imagery, being baptised is like being born, getting married, dying, and having a bath—all at the same time. Which makes it pretty special! There's quite a lot involved behind the scenes.

A wedding

So first, getting baptised is like getting married. A baptism service is like a wedding, except the baptisands (which is what you call someone who is going to get baptised), do not marry each other, or the minister. They get married to God.

This is clear from the way the Bible talks about baptism. There are lots of places in the New Testament which talk about this. But let's turn to Acts. It's the Day of Pentecost and Peter is preaching about Jesus and the resurrection. He says:

> "'Therefore let all Israel be assured of this: God has made this Jesus, whom you crucified, both Lord and Messiah.' When the people heard this, they were cut to the heart and said to Peter and the other apostles, 'Brothers, what shall we do?' Peter replied, 'Repent and be baptized, every one of you, in the name of Jesus Christ for the forgiveness of your sins. And you will receive the gift of the Holy Spirit. The promise is for you and your children and for all who are far off—for all whom the Lord our God will call.' With many other words he warned them; and he pleaded with them, 'Save yourselves from this corrupt generation.' Those who accepted his message were baptised, and about three thousand were added to their number that day." (Acts 2:36-41)

The first thing here is that God calls people to himself, and for himself. He wants them. God's promises are for all whom God calls to himself. Getting baptised is saying, therefore, that God has got you. Being baptised in the name of Jesus Christ says you belong to Jesus Christ. I am his and he is mine.

The New Testament puts it in other ways too. So the Apostle Paul says in Galatians 3:27 that if you've been baptised into Christ you have "put on Christ", as if he was a jumper or a coat or a special robe you can wear. But all these different ways of speaking are getting at one main point: if you're baptised in the name of Jesus, you belong to him. You're united together. You're a couple, like being married, except this marriage is not just "till death do us part." It lasts forever.

So that's the first thing. Baptism is like a wedding. In baptism, God says he wants you, so you belong to Jesus. Of course, it's even better than that really. If you belong to Jesus, he belongs to you as well. Plus, as in every marriage, what's his is yours, and what's yours is his. That means you have access to all the privileges of the Son of God—like access to God the Father in heaven. And he has access to every part of your life. Which is a little more sobering, isn't it? Baptism says I belong to Jesus.

Another interesting thing about this marriage is that Jesus isn't single when he marries us. He is already married to millions of other Christians too. Just like when you get married you inherit all your spouse's family, Jesus brings his family with him into his new marriage with us. That is, in baptism we are also made a part of his church, his people. As 1 Corinthians 12:13 puts it, we were "baptised into one body." So we're not just baptised into a one-to-one with Jesus, but into a whole new family.

A funeral

The second thing, is that a baptism service is also like a funeral. Baptism is meant to be symbolic of death and resurrection.

So if we are baptised into Jesus, we die and rise again with Jesus. That's why it is such a dramatic picture. As we're plunged down into the water, so to speak, the symbolism is that we're dying. When we come up again for air, we live again—just as Jesus died on the cross and then on the third day he rose again. Except in church we don't keep you under water for three days. That would be a little bit excessive. Sometimes it's just a symbolic splash.

To see this in the Bible, let's turn to Romans 6:1-4.

> *"What shall we say, then? Shall we go on sinning so that grace may increase? By no means! We are those who have died to sin; how can we live in it any longer? Or don't you know that all of us who were baptized into Christ Jesus were baptized into his death? We were therefore buried with him through baptism into death in order that, just as Christ was raised from the dead through the glory of the Father, we too may live a new life."*

Paul says if we have been baptised into Christ, then we have been baptised into his *death*. So the baptism service is like a funeral. But what is it that dies? Obviously it could be you if the minister did keep you under the water for three days. But what does Paul say? He says, in verse 6, "we know that our old self was crucified with him so that the body ruled by sin might be done away with, that we should no longer be slaves to sin." Our old self was crucified. That is, our sinful self, our rebellious nature.

So being baptised is about God killing your sinful nature. God killed me so I'm dead to sin, as Romans 6:11 puts it. We're to consider ourselves dead to sin. As if sin was some ugly monster inside us which controlled us and told us what to do. But now that we're united to Jesus, which is symbolised in baptism, that little monster is dead.

So don't listen to it anymore. When we hear sin saying, "Go on, you know you want to"—to something you know God wouldn't want you to do—then we can say, "No. I was baptised into Christ's death. Sin is dead, and has no power over me. I'm not going to do it."

A birthday

The flip side of this is in Romans 6:4. If we're united in Jesus's death, we're also united in Jesus's resurrection. That is, we live a new life. Or as Paul puts it, we walk in newness of life. That means a baptism is like a birthday party too. It's all about celebrating my new life in Christ.

God raised me so I live a new life. I'm now able to live like Jesus, to say "no" to sin and "yes" to good things. And one day, as Romans 6:5 says, I will enjoy a resurrection like Jesus's resurrection. When I die that's not the end. There's more—so much more.

So a baptism is like a wedding in that it is about a new and intimate relationship with Jesus. It's like a funeral because we're baptised into his death, and we're dead to sin. And it's like a birthday party because we're also baptised into Jesus's resurrection and can live a new life.

A bath

Finally, baptism is, unsurprisingly, like a bath.

When I say it's like a bath, I mean, it actually *is* a bath sometimes! Literally when people are baptised in many churches they are plunged down into a big tub of water. Even if it's more like a sprinkling in some churches, baptism is clearly symbolic of being washed and cleansed. Cleansed from what? From the filth and the dirt and the bad smell of sin.

We can see this in Acts 2 where we started. Peter says in Acts 2:38, "Repent and be baptized, every one of you, in the name of Jesus Christ for the forgiveness of your sins." Baptism is related to the forgiveness of our sins. A few chapters later in Acts 22:16, we can see this connection even more clearly. There, Paul is telling people about how he became a Christian. Someone said to him, "And now what are you waiting for? Get up, be baptised and wash your sins away, calling on his name."

Do you see how he relates baptism and washing away your sins? Just as having a bath washes away the dirt on our bodies, so baptism is a sign of God washing away the dirt in our souls. Because every time we *do* something or *think* something or *say* something which offends God, it's like it stains us. It makes us dirty before him. So much so that God says even our righteous acts are like filthy rags before him. Our sins are like scarlet, which need to be washed as white as snow (Isaiah 1:18).

We like to think that we can do good things to please God. When my children were quite young, they were very proud when they did a poo on the potty. They would jump up and come running in to see us, announcing the fact with great delight, and calling us to "Come and see!" Lovely. Well, as far as God is concerned, if we're not right with him then everything we do is like that. We say, "Look God, I don't believe in Jesus and stuff but look, I give to charity. Look, I was nice to that old lady who was trying to cross the road. I work hard at school. Come and see how I never rebel against my parents. Look at all the recycling I do and organic vegetables I eat. Come and be impressed by my great deeds of righteousness."

As far as God is concerned, that's like holding out a piece of used toilet paper and offering it to him as if it was something special. It's like calling him to look at a big poo in the potty and expecting him to be ecstatic, and reward us. Now, it's actually quite good that a 3 year old can do that. But you get my point? Our sin, our rebellion against God, and even our good works do not impress God. They stink. They make us dirty.

In our heart of hearts we feel it. We know when we've done something wrong. It gives us a sick feeling in the pit of our stomachs and it can make us feel unclean, wrong, stained, spoilt. And yet God offers to wash us clean of all that. He offers forgiveness of all our sins through Jesus.

Actually what makes us clean is his blood shed on the cross. It seems strange that blood would make us clean. If you've ever had a nose bleed or something like that you'll know that blood is very hard to wash out of clothes. But Jesus's blood washes away all the stains of sin, because he shed his blood in our place. He took the punishment for all our sin so that we don't have to suffer for it ourselves. And if God looks at us and sees us covered in that blood, so to speak, he knows that he doesn't have to punish us. Someone has already died for our sins, and God doesn't punish the same sins twice.

Baptism reminds us of all this. It is a vivid picture of washing away the dirt of sin. Just as when you have a bath water seeps into every nook and cranny and soaks us, so God washes away all our sin, every last bit, even the things we're too ashamed to mention.

An outward physical sign

So, I said at the start that baptism is the outward and physical sign of an inward and spiritual grace. It's a visible picture of an invisible present. Well, these are the presents: baptism is about God giving us a wedding present, a funeral present, a birthday present, and a bath. It's about the gift of union with Christ, so that I get my hands on his righteousness, his purity, and perfection. And I'm washed clean of my sins and forgiven.

So those are the presents. That's what baptism represents. But what about the outward physical sign? What about the visible picture? How does it actually *work?* Historically there have been three main answers to that question.

Is it automatic?

First, we could say baptism works automatically. Actually getting baptised, some claim, is what does the trick. Being splashed with that special water by a specially authorised person and having specially authorised words spoken over you will automatically confer upon you all these gifts of God. It's automatic. So everyone who has been baptised is made spiritually one with Jesus, and can look forward to going to heaven one day having had all their sins forgiven. Baptism is what makes you a Christian. It's essential, and it works automatically.

There are some obvious difficulties with that view. Not least of which is that if you look at those who have been baptised, they don't all live as if they were born again. And of course the Bible does seem to indicate that what you really need is *faith*, not baptism. It's trusting in Jesus, having faith in what he says and relying on what he's done—that's what saves us. Not just taking part in a ritual ceremony.

So I don't think there's any biblical evidence to support an automatic view of baptism, as if it was a magical Harry Potter type spell or something. If it was, I guess we could evangelise the world by filling up a few fire engines with holy water and sprinkling every passer by!

Is it symbolic?

Some people go to the opposite extreme then and say that baptism is purely symbolic. It's just a symbol and doesn't actually do anything. It makes no difference at all, it's just a visual aid.

Now, we have to be careful with that, because obviously it *is* a visual aid. A really good visual aid, designed by God himself to illustrate what he does for those who trust in Jesus. It's a visual aid of him uniting us to Jesus, and of giving us a spiritual bath. But is that all it is?

I don't think so. I think that if the Bible insists we get baptised then it must be more significant than a mere visual aid. If it was just a visual aid then we could just watch it happen to someone else, couldn't we? Why do we have to do it ourselves?

The Bible is clear on this. Jesus said at the end of Matthew's Gospel that his disciples should go and make disciples of all nations, *baptising* them in the name of the Father, the Son, and the Holy Spirit, and teaching them to obey everything he commanded (Matthew 28:19-20). So baptism, mentioned first there *before* teaching, is clearly important to Jesus. It doesn't make us born again automatically—believing and trusting in Jesus does that—but it is obviously something Jesus wants every Christian to do, as a matter of obedience to him. I think that's because it actually does something.

Symbol and Right

So the third option, is that baptism is a symbol that gives us certain rights and privileges.

So, yes it's a symbol of all that God promises us in the good news of Jesus. But also, being baptised gives us the right to claim God's promises. It entitles us to an inheritance. So it's saying, this person standing here soaking wet, is entitled to eternal life, forgiveness of sins, a relationship with Jesus. They are baptised into Jesus's name, and so they are allowed to claim all the privileges of Jesus. It's like a passport into God's kingdom.

Now let me be clear on this. It doesn't get us into God's kingdom on its own. Believing and trusting in Jesus does that. But being baptised as Jesus commanded is the sign that I am a member of that kingdom and can claim all the privileges of membership if I want to.

I think something actually happens when we get baptised, in the way that something actually happens when a couple get married and say those words to each other, "I will." They begin a new relationship. They are legally entering into a covenant with each other. And when we are baptised that's exactly what we are doing with God—officially entering into a covenant with him.

Now, I may be unfaithful to that covenant. That happens in marriages sometimes of course, and it happens when people are baptised into the covenant too. People can be unfaithful. But if I am baptised—in an arranged marriage as a baptised infant or as an adult who has come to faith later in life—either way, I am under an obligation to repent and believe and obey Christ. I am in a covenant with him.

So baptism in and of itself doesn't help me unless I grab hold of its benefits by faith. Faith is the magic ingredient, as it were, which activates the privileges of baptism.

That means, of course, that if I get baptised but don't actually believe in Jesus then it does me no good at all. I have the promise and I'm entitled to all sorts of goodies like forgiveness and eternal life, but I never actually exercise my faith in Jesus and go to claim those things. It's like being the heir to a huge fortune, having a certificate which says, "This person is entitled to 1 million pounds"... but never actually going to the bank to collect.

Which actually makes me worse off. If I'm baptised, I'm privileged. So if I don't take advantage of that privilege and cash in the promises of God, then I will be judged by God one day for being ungrateful. And I will also be judged for not keeping the covenant which I have entered into by being baptised.

Infant Baptism

Now this brings us to the tricky issue of infant baptism. Maybe we can see how all this applies to those who are baptised as adults. They profess to be Christians and to have trusted in Jesus. But what about those who were baptised as infants? Is that the same? Is that still valid? Why do babies get splashed? And if I was splashed as a baby but I've only recently had a conversion experience or only just started to live like a Christian, do I need to get baptised again, "properly" as it were?

Not everyone will agree on this. Which is OK. We're allowed to disagree on some issues without getting into a fight about it. But the overwhelming majority of Christians in the world today, and the overwhelming majority of Christians who have ever lived in fact, all baptise their kids. What's the thinking behind that?

Well, since the time of Abraham, about 4000 years ago, God's people have been given a sign of admission into his covenant family. In the Old Testament the sign was circumcision, for boys and men at least. Quite painful, and not a great thing to think about for too long if you're male. But that was the sign that you were part of God's family in the Old Testament. In the New Testament, baptism is now the sign of being part of God's people. Which is a lot less painful, I assure you. Better to be splashed than slashed!

God said to Abraham in Genesis chapter 17 that circumcision was a sign of the promises God had made to Abraham. It was an outward physical sign of an inward spiritual reality, just as baptism is. And God said those promises were for Abraham and also for his children (Genesis 17:7). Hence the children of believers were circumcised as babies under the Old Covenant. They would need to have faith as they grew up of course, to cash in the promises. But they were to be given the sign, eight days after they were born.

Now that Christ has come, children of believers under the *New* Covenant may receive baptism in the same way because, as the Apostle Peter says in Acts chapter 2, "the promise is for you and for your children." The same words as God said to Abraham. So infant baptism is the same as infant circumcision. It's an outward sign of an inward spiritual reality.

The spiritual reality is the same in both cases: both circumcision and baptism are about being part of a covenant with God, part of God's plans and promises, being forgiven, and living for God. It's just that the actual physical sign has changed, and girls can now receive it as well.

Infant baptism and adult baptism are the same in essence. Neither adult nor infant baptism do us any good, unless the person being baptised trusts in Jesus at some point and cashes in the promises. It's just that with infants, the faith comes after the sign whereas with adults, it usually comes before.

But not always. Sometimes people are baptised as adults or as teenagers but they don't actually believe in it all, not really. And then a few years later they are born again as they trust in Jesus. We don't then say to them, "Oh well, you've got to get baptised *again*." Just as we wouldn't say to a husband who suddenly starts to actually appreciate his wife after years of neglect, that he has to get married to her again. It doesn't matter what order it happens in. What matters is that we believe in Jesus and are baptised.

So if you were baptised as an infant, like me—that's great. And if you start trusting in Jesus at some point as you grow up—like I did—that's great. But you don't need to get re-baptised just because there's a time lag. Your baptism was valid and real the first time, if it was baptism in the name of Jesus or baptism in the name of the Father, the Son, and the Holy Spirit. As Ephesians 4 says, we believe in "one baptism", not repeated baptisms every time I think something important has happened to me spiritually. We're probably going to have spiritual growth spurts for the rest of our lives.

What those of us who were baptised as babies need to do is appreciate what God gave to us in that baptism. And as we appreciate all the gifts symbolised in our baptism, we need to appropriate them, grab hold of them, take them for ourselves, by believing and trusting in Jesus. The idea behind the service of Confirmation, is that someone baptised earlier (often as an infant) gets a chance to publicly confirm that they really do believe and trust in Jesus, just as their parents and godparents promised they would bring them up to do. It's a chance for them to stand up and be counted as a

Christian when they are ready to do that for themselves, and be recognised as such by the wider church.

So whenever someone is baptised or confirmed, we should all celebrate. And we should remember our own baptism if we can, or appreciate the significance of our own baptism if we can't recall it. It's an outward physical sign of an inward spiritual grace, given to us by Jesus for our good.

Questions for Reflection

1. Why might it be important that a child's parents are themselves practising Christians before they think about having their child baptised?

2. How might infant baptism testify to the priority of God's grace in the Christian life?

3. Why do people often give their "testimony" at Confirmation services?

Prayer

Almighty God,
who gives the gift of the Holy Spirit
to all who repent and believe the gospel:
grant in your mercy that we may not be ashamed
to confess the faith of Christ crucified,
and to fight valiantly against sin, the world, and the devil
as his faithful soldiers and servants,
until the end of our lives;
for we ask in the name of Jesus,
who was raised from death by your glory
that we may walk in newness of life.
Amen.

The Lord's Supper

Lee Gatiss

"Then came the day of Unleavened Bread on which the Passover lamb had to be sacrificed. Jesus sent Peter and John, saying, 'Go and make preparations for us to eat the Passover.' 'Where do you want us to prepare for it?' they asked. He replied, 'As you enter the city, a man carrying a jar of water will meet you. Follow him to the house that he enters, and say to the owner of the house, "The Teacher asks: Where is the guest room, where I may eat the Passover with my disciples?" He will show you a large room upstairs, all furnished. Make preparations there.' They left and found things just as Jesus had told them. So they prepared the Passover.

When the hour came, Jesus and his apostles reclined at the table. And he said to them, 'I have eagerly desired to eat this Passover with you before I suffer. For I tell you, I will not eat it again until it finds fulfilment in the kingdom of God.' After taking the cup, he gave thanks and said, 'Take this and divide it among you. For I tell you I will not drink again from the fruit of the vine until the kingdom of God comes.' And he took bread, gave thanks and broke it, and gave it to them, saying, 'This is my body given for you; do this in remembrance of me.'

In the same way, after the supper he took the cup, saying, 'This cup is the new covenant in my blood, which is poured out for you.'"

Luke 22:7-20

In this chapter, we're going to look at another aspect of our corporate life together: the Lord's Supper. That's the name given in Scripture itself to the meal Christians often share in church. It's also known as Holy Communion, or just Communion.

The Supper is a wonderful thing, instituted by Jesus himself as a comfort and a help for us, to nurture and strengthen our faith. There has been, however, a great deal of debate and confusion surrounding it over the centuries. So it is very important that in this area of our corporate life, as with any other, we get our thinking on it clear.

Preaching is about hearing. But the Lord's Supper is about eating and drinking—and looking, in various directions.

Looking back

First, in the Lord's Supper we *look back* to our salvation achieved by Christ on the cross. The focus of the Lord's Supper is the cross where Jesus died. As Paul says in 1 Corinthians 11:26, in the Lord's Supper, "we proclaim the Lord's *death*." Indeed, when Jesus first instituted this meal, it was called the *Last* Supper, because it was the last meal Jesus had with his disciples before he died.

Now, the Last Supper was a Passover meal, as we can see in the reading at the start of this chapter. The Passover meal originally commemorated the Passover, something that happened to God's people in the book of Exodus. At the time of Moses, God said he was going to judge everyone in Egypt by killing, in one night, all the first-born sons. The only way to escape was for a family to kill a lamb, eat it together, and smear its blood on the lintel and door-posts of the house. Then the destroying angel would *pass-over* that house, and the people inside would be safe.

That's just what happened (see Exodus 12). So every year, the people were meant to remember this amazing deliverance by having a Passover meal. Jesus says that the Lord's Supper is like that. Except now, he is the Lamb of God (John 1:29). He is the one who is punished in our place, whose blood is shed, so that we can live and not be judged by God. The original Passover was just a small picture of the greater reality that we find at the cross.

The Passover, and all the other animal sacrifices we find in the Old Testament, were part of the Old Covenant. They needed priests and altars and that sort of thing. Jesus says he is beginning the New Covenant. We know from the prophet Jeremiah, that the New Covenant is about how we can all know God directly, without the need for human mediators or priests, having the law written on our hearts:

> "'The days are coming', declares the LORD,
>> 'when I will make a new covenant
>> with the people of Israel
>> and with the people of Judah.
> It will not be like the covenant
> I made with their ancestors
>> when I took them by the hand
>> to lead them out of Egypt,
>> because they broke my covenant,
>> though I was a husband to them',
>> declares the LORD.
> 'This is the covenant I will make with the people of Israel
>> after that time', declares the LORD.
> 'I will put my law in their minds
>> and write it on their hearts.
> I will be their God,
>> and they will be my people.
> No longer will they teach their neighbour,
>> or say to one another, "Know the LORD",
>> because they will all know me,

> *from the least of them to the greatest',*
> *declares the* Lord.
> 'For I will forgive their wickedness*
> *and will remember their sins no more.'"*
>
> (Jeremiah 31:31-34)

So we mustn't get the wrong idea about this meal we share together. It is not about a priest sacrificing Jesus again on an altar. All that business of priests and sacrifices and altars has been fulfilled in Jesus. He died once-and-for-all to put an end to it, and to open up a new covenant (see Hebrews 9-10). We all have access to God now, through our one great high priest, Jesus. And he himself was the perfect lamb of God, sacrificed once-and-for-all on the cross. We remember this by having a meal at a table, not by going backwards in time and bringing in all that priestly-sacrifice-altar stuff.

So the first thing we need to notice from Scripture is that the Lord's Supper is all about the death of Jesus. When we eat and drink together, *we look back to the cross* and what Christ did for us there. It makes us rejoice that he did everything that was necessary to save us. He can save to the uttermost all those who come to God through him (Hebrews 7:25).

Looking forward

We look back to our salvation achieved by Christ on the cross, but in the Lord's Supper we also look *forward* to an assured future with Christ at the heavenly feast.

All the passages in the Gospels which describe the Last Supper show Jesus talking about the coming of the kingdom of God. In a sense the kingdom is already with us, because King Jesus has come. But his kingdom will come in its fullness when Jesus comes again, and everything and everyone submits to his rule. At the name of Jesus, every knee will bow and everyone will say, "Yes! He's the King. He's the Lord" (see Philippians 2:10-11).

That is what we are looking forward to. Because the way Jesus describes it, it's going to be terrific. Jesus's parables often compare life in the kingdom to a huge party. He calls it a great feast, or a great banquet. So this is what we're looking forward to when Jesus comes again. As Paul says in 1 Corinthians 11, in the Supper we proclaim the Lord's death "until he comes"—until he comes again and it is all finally fulfilled.

So we not only *look back* when we eat and drink together, we *look forward* too. If Jesus has died for us, then we have no worries about our place at the banquet. We are invited—all we must do is come.

It's not like going round for dinner at a friend's house—Jesus doesn't want us to bring anything in return! We don't need to earn our place at the feast, or pay for it somehow, or bring our good works with us to show off at the party. If we did try to bring something, that would just be saying that the feast wasn't good enough. And that would be an insult to the King, wouldn't it?

So coming to the Lord's Supper together is a foretaste of heaven. We are invited, we accept, we receive from our host, and humbly take what he offers us. It is just a foretaste—a little bit of bread, a tiny sip of wine. But it should make us smile as we remember what it points forward to, what we will enjoy when God's kingdom comes in its fullness.

Some people get terribly worked up about it. "Am I really good enough for this?" they ask, "I feel unworthy to come to such a meal." And the answer to that is, "No, you're not good enough. You're not worthy." Nobody is. No-one is good enough for God. And so no-one is good enough to eat at the Lord's Table, or even to pick up the crumbs from under his table.

But the glory of the gospel is that Jesus invites us to come even though we are not good enough. We might be "looking down" at our feet in shame, thinking only of our sin. But Jesus tells us to look back instead at what he did for us on the cross. Our sin has been paid for and dealt with. God didn't wait for the world to reform itself before he sent his Son to die. And anyway, if you wait until you are good enough you'll wait forever.

So we come to the Lord's Supper looking back at the cross in gratitude for what Jesus did for us there. And we come looking forward to the great feast in heaven, knowing that what Jesus did for us guarantees our place there. The Supper feeds us in such a way as to leave us hungry for real food at that heavenly banquet, while also assuring us that we will indeed share in that. We won't be there because we deserve to be. We'll be there because he's a gracious and loving master. And for that same reason, we can gather around his table, in anticipation of that great day.

Looking around

So far, we've thought about the past and future elements of the Supper. So now, let's turn to the present. When we celebrate communion together, we look around as we share with our brothers and sisters in Christ. But Paul also has a word of rebuke for one of the churches he was involved with. He said:

"So then, when you come together, it is not the Lord's Supper you eat, for when you are eating, some of you go ahead with your own private suppers. As a result, one person remains hungry and another gets drunk. Don't you have homes to eat and drink in? Or do you despise the church of God by humiliating those who have nothing? What shall I say to you? Shall I praise you? Certainly not in this matter!

For I received from the Lord what I also passed on to you: The Lord Jesus, on the night he was betrayed, took bread, and when he had given thanks, he broke it and said, 'This is my body, which is for you; do this in remembrance of me.' In the same way, after supper he took the cup, saying, 'This cup is the new covenant in my blood; do this, whenever you drink it, in re-membrance of me.' For whenever you eat this bread and drink this cup, you proclaim the Lord's death until he comes.

So then, whoever eats the bread or drinks the cup of the Lord in an unworthy manner will be guilty of sinning against the body and blood of the Lord. Everyone ought to examine themselves before they eat of the bread and drink from the cup. For those who eat and drink without discerning the body of Christ eat and drink judgment on themselves. That is why many among you are weak and sick, and a number of you have fallen asleep. But if we were more discerning with regard to ourselves, we would not come under such judgment. Nevertheless, when we are judged in this way by the Lord, we are being disciplined so that we will not be finally condemned with the world.

So then, my brothers and sisters, when you gather to eat, you should all eat together. Anyone who is hungry should eat some-thing at home, so that when you meet together it may not result in judgment." (1 Corinthians 11:20-34)

The Lord's Supper is not just an individual thing. I don't just come for "my communion" as some people like to put it. It's meant to be a corporate thing, a team activity, a family meal. We do it together as a body. And so we must be very careful about our relationships within the body, within the church.

In Corinth they had lots of divisions. They were a selfish bunch, at odds with each other and not paying much attention to the needs of others in the congregation. Paul says in this passage that their Communion services do more harm than good. Why? Be-cause they are priestly, High Church affairs? No. Paul's criticism is something which applies much more broadly than that. He says their celebrations of the Lord's Supper do more harm than good because they are neglecting this corporate aspect of what it's all about.

According to 1 Corinthians 10:17, "Because there is one loaf, we, who are many, are one body, for we all share the one loaf." Are we selfish, divisive, at odds with others? If so, we need to sort that out before we come to church, *especially* if we're going to celebrate the Lord's Supper together. By eating and drinking together we are saying that we are brothers and sisters in Christ, one body. But by fighting and gossiping and holding grudges against each other we are denying that. By looking down on fellow members of the body of Christ, the Church, we sin against Christ himself.

That's what it means when Paul says, "For those who eat and drink without discerning the body of Christ eat and drink judgment on themselves" (1 Corinthians 11:29). We must recognise that we are the body of Christ—one body, together, and not divide it in any way. So, a rich man and a poor man can eat together at this table if they are both Christians: wealth does not matter. A young woman and an old woman can eat together at this table because age doesn't matter. As the old song puts it, "Red and yellow, black and white, all are precious in his sight."

But Paul warns us that if we are causing strife and discord within the body, then we had better *not* eat and drink. So we need in a sense to "look inwards" here too, to examine ourselves and see if we are causing disharmony. Have we forgiven that person in the row behind us for what they said last week? Or are we harbouring grudges? Have we done something against that person on the other side of the church, and not confessed it or put it right? Then we need to sort these things out before we eat the Supper together.

In some churches they have "the peace" before they share the supper, for this very reason. It's not supposed to be just about shaking hands with everybody or sharing "holy hugs." It's supposed to be to make sure we are at peace with everyone we are about to share the Supper with. Not every church does liturgical handshaking, but that doesn't make it any less important to be right with one another before we share the supper together.

If we don't sort ourselves out in terms of our relationships, we only make things worse for ourselves. That's what 1 Corinthians 11:30 says. The Corinthians thought it wouldn't make any difference whether they had right relationships with others in the church. But Paul says, "That is why many among you are weak and sick, and a number of you have fallen asleep." *Some have died!* It is a dangerous thing to take Communion together and yet deny that we are one family by the way we act towards God or each other. A very dangerous thing.

Looking up

So we look back, we look forward and we look around as we share the Lord's Supper together. Finally, then, we also look up. We look up at Christ and feed on him in our hearts by faith.

At its simplest, the Supper teaches us that just as our bodies are nourished by bread and wine, so our souls are nourished by Christ. We feed ourselves with bread to keep our bodies healthy. In the same way we must feed on Christ to keep our souls healthy. He is the only source of spiritual sustenance that will do that. We participate in him: "Is not the cup of thanksgiving for which we give thanks a participation in the blood of Christ? And is not the bread that we break a participation in the body of Christ?" (1 Corinthians 10:16) By eating and drinking this bread and this wine, we participate in Christ, we feed on him.

Now, how on earth do we feed on Christ? Are we cannibals? Certainly not! We don't call Jesus down from heaven so we can tear bits off him for food. Jesus's literal flesh and blood are seated at the right hand of the Father in heaven. Jesus hasn't moved from there for the last 2000 years, and he's not coming back until he comes again "to judge the living and the dead" (as we saw in the Creed).

At the Last Supper Jesus did say, "This is my body" as he handed out the bread. But everyone could see that it wasn't *literally* his body they were eating. If it was, he was eating himself too, which is very odd indeed!

So if the bread isn't literally Jesus, is he perhaps *in* the bread and wine somehow? Like water is *in* a sponge maybe? Again, certainly not! His actual body and blood are in heaven, seated at the right hand of the Father. Jesus can't be in two places at once, any more than you or I can. Why not? Because he has a real physical human body. The same kind of body as you or I have. That was the point—at the first Christmas he really did become just like one of us, so he could represent us, and die in our place.

So how do we participate in him, or feed on him? Is it just symbolic? I don't think so. Something real actually happens when we eat and drink. If it was merely a visual aid, why are some people sick and dying in Corinth because they are taking communion wrongly, as we have seen? It must be more than a visual aid mustn't it? Otherwise, why doesn't the minister just do everything up front in church so others can all see, and leave it at that? If it was just a symbolic visual aid you'd need a good view, but you wouldn't need to actually take part. Yet Jesus insists we take part: Eat, he says, and drink.

Jesus wants us not just to look at the bread and smell the wine, but to taste it ourselves and drink it in. It's all about participation and "appropriation"—actually taking it on board for ourselves. And we do that spiritually, by faith. It's all by faith. So we *trust* that as we eat, we truly feed on Christ. It relies on faith because we can't actually see or taste any difference. But something real happens:

+ Either, we eat and drink and feed on Christ in our hearts by faith with thanksgiving, for our comfort and spiritual nourishment.

+ Or, we eat and drink our own condemnation as some in Corinth were doing.

The difference between them is faith—do we actually believe and trust and follow Jesus, or not?

Now let's not be confused. In the Supper, we feed on Christ in the same way we feed on him when we hear and submit to his word. We're getting the same spiritual sustenance—it's just that rather than being a listening experience only, the Supper is physical: smell, taste, touch. In the sermon, Christ appeals to our ears, minds, and hearts; in the Supper he appeals through our eyes, hands, mouths, and other senses. It is just a different form of preaching.

One final point about looking up. Some people think the Holy Spirit needs to come down and change the bread and wine we use. Their prayers around the table sometimes ask the Spirit to do just that. But I think that actually what happens is that the Spirit (who lives within every believing Christian) works within us, and by his power we are able to feed on Christ. We don't call Christ down to be here with us, and we don't call the Spirit down to change anything. No, Christ calls us to *look up*—to "lift up our hearts"—and to feed on him by faith, in the power of the Spirit who already dwells within us.

Take and Eat!

There are lots of other questions and issues which surround this simple meal. How often should we take communion together, for instance, and what kind of bread should we use? Should there be a non-alcoholic wine and a gluten-free bread option? We haven't got space to look into all these things, and churches do things differently.

What we most need to remember is that this isn't magic. It's not about getting a God-Smartie that works regardless of our faith. It is of no benefit to us at all if we do not believe and trust in Jesus. To take part in the Lord's Supper and yet to reject Jesus's authority over our lives is in fact sacrilege. It's disrespecting the King.

Eating and drinking together without actually loving Jesus is like being invited to dinner at the house of someone you actually hate and despise. You accept the invitation but when you get there you trash the place, say rude things about your host, or ignore him. Well, if you did that at any other supper party, what would your host do? Ultimately, he'd throw you out.

That's why those who can't confirm that they are Christians, and openly accept Jesus's rule and authority over their lives, should not come to the table. Taking part in the Lord's Supper is an act of faith—we say "yes, we believe", and, "yes we want to be a part of this and follow Jesus as our Lord, though we know that we are unworthy so much as to gather up the crumbs under his table." And we shouldn't say that, either out loud or by eating and drinking the bread and wine, unless we really mean it.

Questions for Reflection

1. Do you think someone should be baptised and confirmed before taking the Lord's Supper? Why, or why not?

2. Why is it dangerous to take the Lord's Supper if one is not a practising Christian?

3. Why is the Lord's Supper more than just a visual aid?

Prayer

God our Father,
who gives us all good things, richly to enjoy:
grant that as we celebrate the Lord's Supper together,
we might feed on Christ in our hearts by faith
and look forward to the heavenly kingdom
of the one who through the eternal Spirit
offered himself without blemish to God
and is seated at your right hand on high;
For we ask in his precious name,
Amen.

The Church

Ash Carter

What does Church mean?

Should it be *a* church or *the* church? It rather depends. We might say, "there is a church over there," meaning a church building. We might refer to a particular organisation, such as the Church of Scientology, the Unitarian Church, the Church of Jesus Christ of Latter Day Saints, or the Church of Wittertainment (google it).

And not one of these is what the Bible means by "church." Nor, strictly speaking, is the Church of England, but we'll get to that. If we go to a dictionary for a definition of the church, we might get all of these. But God didn't give us a dictionary, he gave us the Bible. So let's ask a more precise question.

The word "church" in the Bible

In the Old Testament, the focus is not so much on the place where people gather as the *assembly*, the people gathered together to God. This can happen at Sinai, or the tabernacle in the wilderness, or at the temple. In each place, this is where God is present and that is where the people of God do church—they assemble to God.

By the time of the New Testament, the Jews were scattered all over the ancient world, and meeting houses had sprung up so that they could gather together. We now know those buildings as *synagogues*, but the word synagogue literally means *gather together*. The focus is still on the people of God, gathering for worship.

As Christians became distinct from the body of Judaism, they began to gather away from the synagogue, and the Bible takes a new word to describe them: *ekklesia*. The *Church*. But the word *ekklesia* still means a gathering called together. So in Acts 19:39, it is used of the "lawful assembly"—the gathering of the people of Ephesus to determine civil policy. The New Testament writers have taken a word in common use and given it a profound new meaning.

Already, then, we can see why it isn't helpful to use the word "church" about a building. The church is what happens (hopefully) within the building. But what about our other uses of the word "church"? Are they right or wrong? Again, we need to go back to the Bible to see how the word is used. That will give us our parameters for legitimate use.

The church as the final, heavenly gathering

If we want to talk about church in its purest and completest form, then we have to talk about the church at the resurrection. "But you have come to Mount Zion, to the city of the living God, the heavenly Jerusalem. You have come to thousands upon thousands of angels in joyful assembly, to the church of the firstborn, whose names are written in heaven" (Hebrews 12:22-23a).

Let's start with the location of this church. The heavenly Jerusalem, Mount Zion, the city of the living God; these are references to the New Creation of Revelation 21-22. This is the eternal city. Moreover, the gathering here is both the *assembly* of the angels and the *church* of the firstborn, those who have the status of heirs of the kingdom of God. It is the same body as John describes in Revelation 7:9, "After this I looked, and there before me was a great multitude that no one could count, from every nation, tribe, people and language, standing before the throne and before the Lamb. They were wearing white robes and were holding palm branches in their hands." This is the people of God, gathered together at the end of time.

One crucial final question is this: On what basis are they gathered? Hebrews tells us that their names are written in heaven. Why? What makes them so secure that their names are inked into the ledgers of heaven before they even arrive? They have washed their robes and made them white in the blood of the Lamb (Revelation 7:14). This is not a method for cleaning your clothes that I recommend. But it is a method of cleaning your soul. The language recalls the Passover lamb, slaughtered in the place of the people. Here, it is Jesus, slaughtered in our place, suffering the death that we deserve for our sin. We are to wash our robes, ourselves, in Jesus's blood. We are to trust him, to depend on him.

This church, then, is all the people throughout history and from across the world who have trusted Jesus, gathered together into the greatest megachurch you can imagine.

The global church

Since the church at its most fundamental is all the believers from all time, many of them have gone on to be with Christ. We might therefore expect the New Testament to speak of the church as a global, earthly reality. There are times when there is clearly an earthly focus, but the church is not *exclusively* the earthly entity (Matthew 16:18; Ephesians 1:22). One text that certainly tends this way is 1 Timothy 3:14-15, where Paul says, "I am writing you these instructions so that, if I am delayed, you will know how people ought to conduct themselves in God's household, which is the church of the living God, the pillar and foundation of the truth."

Here, the church is pictured holding up and holding out the

truth about Jesus. Clearly this is an earthly, not heavenly reality. Yet this seems also to take in all Christians everywhere, rather than just those in a particular place.

One particular variation on this is the description in Acts 9:31: "the church throughout Judea, Galilee and Samaria enjoyed a time of peace and was strengthened." We might think this means that the Bible talks of regional churches but, in light of Acts 1:8, we need to see that this *is* the global church. The gospel had spread throughout Judea, Galilee, and Samaria, and so had the church. That is all the church that there was on earth.

The one true church has one true manifestation all over the world. It is all the people in the world who trust in Jesus alone for their salvation.

The local church

At the other end of the spectrum, the word "church" is also used of the *local* gathering of God's people. So Paul writes "to the church of God in Corinth" (1 Corinthians 1:2) and Jesus speaks "to the seven churches" in Asia (Revelation 1:11).

As we have seen, not every gathering can be called church, not even when it is in a church building. The Zumba class that meets in your hall on a Thursday night is (quite emphatically) not a church, even if your minister goes along. Paul reminds us that it is only the church *of God* that gets to be called a church. This is enormously important for navigating the various other uses of the word "church."

A little church history

At the risk of being simplistic, it is probably helpful at this point to try to understand how the idea of the church has changed (and changed back again) over the millennia. This is very much going to be a potted history.

Early Councils

As the church spread rapidly in the early years after Jesus's ascension, two related questions would come back again and again. First, how do we relate the local churches to the global church? And, secondly, how do we recognise true from false churches? Anyone who has read Galatians will know that false teaching spread early in the church. Paul is emphatic that there is a teaching which unchurches you (Galatians 1:6). In other words, there was false teaching and so false churches.

Since belonging to the eternal church is what matters, and one joins that church by faith alone in Jesus Christ alone for salvation from sin, it became the mark of the church to uphold biblical teaching against error.

One example of the challenge the church faced was the inclusion of gentiles into a predominantly Jewish church (the issue in Galatians). Did they have to become Jews in order to become Christians? The church settled this matter by calling an ecumenical council in Jerusalem, recorded for us in Acts 15. There "the apostles and elders met to consider this question" (Acts 15:6). In the end, they decide not to impose Judaism on the gentiles (verse 19), since God has converted them without doing that (verse 9).

Over the coming centuries, whenever a new teaching came up which might threaten the integrity of the church, the global church called another ecumenical council to discuss the biblical data and to come to a conclusion about what is, and what is not, orthodox. In this way, the church's theology on matters such as the divinity and humanity of Jesus became clearer and clearer, and certain "churches" were recognised as not being Christian at all.

It is from these gatherings that the various creeds came, as clear and (relatively) simple statements of the faith that all Christians hold to. We still use them today to show our solidarity on those issues with our forefathers in the faith.

Division and reinterpretation

Space prohibits a proper discussion of the divisions between Eastern Orthodox and Western Catholic Christianity. The formal split in 1054 really only formalised a division that had been growing for five centuries. There were political factors to do with the fall of the Roman empire; linguistic issues since the West preferred Latin and the East preferred Greek; and theological differences.

Of particular concern for us here are the constitutional differences. At the initial split in the late fifth century, the West was left with one senior bishop, that in Rome (the East had four). By the mid-seventh century the Pope in Rome began to claim that the true church was that which was in fellowship with himself.

The whole church together had stated, in the Nicene-Constantinopolitan Creed (381), that "I believe... in one holy catholic and apostolic church." The Roman Catholic Church began to interpret this to mean one institutional church. One institutional Roman Catholic church. To be a Christian began to mean having a relationship to the Pope, rather than to Jesus.

In the process, the Roman Catholic Church effectively unchurched everyone who disagreed with them, or who did not satisfy their criteria.

Reformation

The Reformers rediscovered, in their reading of Scripture, that salvation was a matter of faith alone in Christ alone, through God's grace alone, revealed in the Scriptures alone and to the glory of God alone. Each one of these took a sledgehammer to the edifice of Roman Catholicism, as it built so much on the authority and office of the Pope and his councils.

The Reformers restored the Bible and, especially, the ministry of Bible preaching to the heart of Christian worship. After all, if the word of God is not preached, how can anyone hear the gospel and believe in Jesus, and so be added to the true church? As Paul says, "How, then, can they call on the one they have not believed in? And how can they believe in the one of whom they have not heard? And how can they hear without someone preaching to them? And how can anyone preach unless they are sent? As it is written: 'How beautiful are the feet of those who bring good news!'" (Romans 10:14-15)

In many ways, the Protestant understanding of the church (*protesting* the abuses of the Roman Catholic church) was much messier than the Roman. To begin with, a congregation could only really be called a church if the Bible was faithfully taught, and church was conducted according to the Bible. Then, even within a faithful congregation, there would be those who attended but who didn't believe the gospel.

Moreover, it meant that the church was anything but monolithic. It meant that there were likely to be faithful congregations in the Roman Catholic Church, in the Eastern Orthodox Church and, at the same time, there would be false churches among the Lutheran and Reformed churches as well. It could get rather confusing.

Nation states, national churches, and confessions

It is often said that the Reformation happened in England by accident, because Henry VIII wanted rid of Catherine of Aragon and the Pope wouldn't let him. Up to a point, this is true. But it actually misses the political reality across Europe at this time. Nations were forming, and the kings of many nations were asserting their authority against the meddling of the Pope. Even decidedly Catholic countries such as France and Spain pushed the Pope out, whilst remaining Catholic. Henry did much the same.

The rise of the nation state gave rise to the need to settle the religion of each country. And if the Pope was not to have ultimate control of a country, then the buck had to stop with the monarch. So Henry became the supreme head of the Church of England.

It is worth seeing that this is pretty much how every European country was settling things as well. At the Peace of Augsburg, between the Catholic Holy Roman Emperor Charles V and the Lutheran Schmalkaldic League, the principle was established *Cuius regio, eius religio*, essentially the religion of the monarch became the official state religion.

These territorial churches began to put together statements of faith. Like the creeds of the early church, they were intended to bring together the Christians of a region under an orthodox banner, and to help them to discern true churches from false. In England, the *Thirty-nine Articles of Religion*, the *Book of Common Prayer*, the Ordinal (ordination services), and the books of Homilies (sermons) became the confessional standard. However, it is really worth seeing that, in most respects, the Articles map very neatly onto the other Protestant confessions being produced across Europe. The proliferation of statements, far from distinguishing the church in one country from that of another, often acted to show the great common ground between them. In so doing, the Protestant churches were signalling that they welcomed one another as members of the universal church.

English developments

One might legitimately ask why it is, if the national churches are so comprehensive, that the Church of England is not the the *only* church in England. Even here, it is worth noticing that often the differences are to do with the *form* of church that is most faithful to the Bible, rather than great differences over doctrine. For example, the Westminster Standards, which are the foundation documents for most Presbyterian churches, were produced in the main by Anglican ministers.

The Act of Toleration (1689) allowed any broadly Protestant gatherings, and churches sprang up, free from the obligation to do things in a particularly *Anglican* way. In practice, this actually settled the Church of England as it was at the time. But, again, we need to recognise that a proliferation of churches and denominations, as the proliferation of confessional statements, does not mean that the one church of God is divided. The Bible has always recognised local churches. And those local churches have always recognised as faithful brothers and sisters those who hold to biblical standards of doctrine and practice.

So what?

Why should you care? In one sense, I hope this is obvious, but just in case, consider this command from Hebrews: "And let us consider how we may spur one another on towards love and good deeds, not giving up meeting together, as some are in the habit of doing" (Hebrews 10:24-25).

It seems that some of the first readers of Hebrews were inclined to give up publicly gathering with God's people. Perhaps they were embarrassed, ashamed, even in danger of persecution. Perhaps they thought they could go it alone as Christians. They couldn't, and neither can we. Indeed, we are commanded to go be church with God's people. One can hardly be a faithful Christian and ignore this.

So, if we *have* to go to church, where *should* we go? We don't pick a building because it looks like a "church" because, well, it doesn't. The *people* are the church.

Then, a local congregation are only a church if the word of God is faithfully taught. It is the truth about Jesus that makes people Christians. Jesus tells us that his words have to remain in us if we are to remain part of the church (John 15:1-8). This is why preaching that clearly explains and applies the meaning of the biblical text is *so* important.

Of course, if the Bible is central to the life of the church, as well as the church service, then there will be other features. The songs and prayers will be shaped by the Bible. If the church uses a liturgy, that should be shaped by the Bible too. The church will take seriously baptism and the Lord's Supper, discussed in earlier chapters, because Jesus commands us to take them seriously. The church will be friendly, because the Bible shapes us to love new people.

It should be possible to ask the minister of any new church to show you the confessional statements to which they hold. This will enable you to locate the church in relationship to the wider church of God.

Most of all, the church must point you to Jesus and encourage you towards faith in him as the one who died in your place. It is such preaching as this which will sustain your faith in Jesus until we are all gathered together in the church of the firstborn in the city of the living God.

Questions for Reflection

1. What are the most important things to look for in a local church?

2. Why might it be important for churches to reflect the diversity of the area in which they meet?

3. Is it OK just to go to church every month or two? Why, or why not?

Prayer

Heavenly Father,
you have built your people, the church,
on the foundation of the apostles and prophets,
Christ Jesus himself being the cornerstone:
by your Spirit, build us up
and knit us together by your most holy word
so that through us your manifold wisdom might be made known
in the heavenly places,
through Jesus Christ our Saviour,
Amen.

Church Armour

A Short Catechism

Church Armour

A Short Catechism

This catechism was originally published in the nineteenth century as Church Association Tract number 59 by the Revd Dr W. F. Taylor, Vicar of St. Chrysostom's, Everton, Liverpool.

> "The following Catechism, written by the Rev. Dr. Taylor, is in use in several schools in Liverpool, where hundreds of children are learning it. The Catechism will be found very valuable in familiarising the minds of young people with the text of the XXXIX Articles, and furnishing them with answers in the very words of the Church to important questions now raised."

The catechism has been revised and updated by Ros Clarke.

Q1	**Who made you?**	Gen. 1:1, 26
A1	God the Father Almighty, maker of heaven and earth, and of all things visible and invisible.	Job 33:4 Heb. 11:3 Nicene Creed
Q2	**Is there more than one God?**	Mark 12:32
A2	No. There is only one living and true God, everlasting, of infinite power, wisdom, and goodness.	Nehemiah 9:6 Jeremiah 10:10 Article 1

Q3	**How many Persons are there in the Godhead?**	Matthew 28:19
		2 Corinthians 13:14
A3	There are three. In the unity of the Godhead there are three Persons, each with the same substance, power, and eternity: the Father, the Son, and the Holy Spirit.	John 1:1
		Acts 5:3,4
		Article 1
Q4	**Who is Jesus Christ?**	Galatians 4:4
A4	Jesus Christ is the Son of God, who took human nature and was born of the virgin Mary. He truly suffered, was crucified, died, and was buried.	John 1:14
		1 Peter 3:18
		Article 2
Q5	**Why did the Son of God become human, and suffer on the Cross?**	Romans 5:10
		2 Corinthians 5:19
A5	The Son of God became human, and suffered in order to reconcile his Father to us, and be a sacrifice for all our sins.	Hebrews 9:26
		1 John 2:2
		Article 2
Q6	**Where did the soul of Christ go when he died?**	Acts 2:27
		Luke 23:43
A6	The soul of Christ went to the realm of the dead.	Article 3
Q7	**Did Christ's soul remain in the realm of the dead, and his body in the grave?**	1 Corinthians 15:4
		Mark 16:19
		1 Thess 4:16
A7	No. Christ truly rose again from death, body and soul. He ascended into heaven in his physical body and he is seated there until he returns to judge all people on the last day.	Article 4
Q8	**Who is the Holy Spirit?**	John 14:26
A8	The Holy Spirit is the third Person of the Trinity, who proceeds from the Father and the Son. He is truly God.	Acts 5:4
		1 Corinthians 2:10
		Article 5

Q9	**What is the rule of faith?**	Isaiah 8:20
A9	The rule of faith is the Bible, or Holy Scripture, which contains all things necessary for salvation. Anything which is not found in the Bible, or demonstrated by the Bible is not necessary for salvation, and no one should be required to believe it.	2 Timothy 3:15 John 5:39 Deuteronomy 12:32 Revelation 22: 18-19 Article 6
Q10	**Is the Old Testament contrary to the New Testament?**	Hebrew 1:1-2 Luke 24:44
A10	No, the Old Testament is not contrary to the New. In both the Old and New Testaments, everlasting life is offered by Christ, who is the only Mediator between God and Man, being both God and Man.	Acts 26:22 Romans 16:26 Article 7
Q11	**What are the three Creeds?**	Article 8
A11	The three Creeds are the Nicene Creed, the Athanasian Creed, and the Apostles' Creed.	
Q12	**Why should we believe these three Creeds?**	2 Timothy 1:13 Article 8
A11	Because they can be clearly proved from Scripture.	
Q13	**What is original sin?**	Psalm 51:5
A13	Original sin is the corruption and fault of the nature of everyone naturally descended from Adam, by which we are all very far from original righteousness, and are of our own nature inclined to evil.	Romans 3:10-12 Romans 8:7 Article 9

Q14	**Are we able to turn to God of our own will?**	John 6:44 John 15:5
A14	No. The human condition since the fall is such that we cannot turn to faith and calling upon God by our own natural strength and good works.	Ephesians 2:1 Article 10
Q15	**What do we need to turn to God?**	Jeremiah 31:18-19
A15	In order to turn to God, we need the grace of God by Christ going before us to give us the will to do good; and working with us, when we have that good will.	1 Corinthians 15:10 Philippians 2:13 Article 10
Q16	**What is the true doctrine of justification?**	Romans 3:24-25 Romans 5:1, 9, 19
A16	The true doctrine of justification is that we are counted righteous before God only for the merit of our Lord Jesus Christ by faith, and not for our own works or for what we deserve.	2 Corinthians 5:21 Philippians 3:9 Article 11
Q17	**What are good works?**	Philippians 1:11
A17	Good works are the fruits of faith, and follow after justification. They always spring from a true and living faith, so that by them a living faith may be recognised as easily as a tree can be discerned by its fruit.	John 15:4-5 Galatians 5:6 Article 12

Q18	**Are works done before justification good works?**	Isaiah 64:6
		Luke 18:11-14
A18	No. Works done before justification are not properly good works, nor are they pleasing to God, because they do not come from faith in Jesus Christ.	Article 13

Q19	**What is election or predestination?**	Ephesians 1:4
		1 Peter 1:2
A19	Election to life is the eternal purpose of God, whereby he has committed before the beginning of the world to saving those whom he has chosen in Christ.	Romans 8:29-30
		Article 17

Q20	**Can someone be saved by sincere faith in another religion?**	John 3:36
		John 14:6
A20	No one can be saved by sincere faith in any other religion, since salvation is found only in the name of Jesus Christ.	Acts 4:12
		Article 18

Q21	**What is the visible church?**	Acts 2:41, 42, 47
A21	The visible Church of Christ is a congregation of faithful believers, in the which the pure word of God is preached, and the sacraments are administered according to Christ's commands.	1 Corinthians 11:23-25
		1 Timothy 3:15
		Article 19

Q22	**What authority does the church have?**	Acts 15:2,23
		Acts 16:4
A22	The Church has authority to establish liturgy and it has authority in controversies of doctrine. However, the church may not ordain anything contrary to God's word, and nor may it so make one part of Scripture contradict another.	1 Corinthians 14:26, 40
		Galatians 1:8
		Article 20

Q23	**Can a denomination be in error?**	Romans 11:20-22
A23	Yes. The Roman Catholic Church and the Eastern Orthodox Churches are in error, both in matters of liturgy and life, as well as in matters of doctrine.	Revelation 2:14, 16, 20
		Article 19

Q24	**Can a General Council of the church be in error?**	Acts 20:29-30
		Article 21
A24	Yes. General Councils are not infallible, since they are human assemblies, and not every member may be governed by the Spirit and word of God. They may err and sometimes have erred even in the things of God.	

Q25	**Can anyone decide to become a preacher or minister?**	Jeremiah 23:21
		Mark 3:14
A25	No. A person must be called and ordained by the church to become a preacher or minister of the sacraments.	1 Timothy 5:22
		2 Timothy 2:2
		Article 23

Q26	**What is a sacrament?**	Acts 10:47
A26	A sacrament is an outward and visible sign of an inward and spiritual grace given to us. Sacraments were ordained by Christ himself, as a means for us to receive grace and be assured of grace.	1 Corinthians 10:16 Article 25
Q27	**How many sacraments has Christ ordained?**	Matthew 28:19 Luke 22:19-20
A27	Two: Baptism and the Lord's Supper.	Article 25
Q28	**What were the sacraments intended for?**	1 Corinthians 11:23-29
A28	The sacraments were intended to be used, not merely observed. They are only effective in those who receive them by faith.	Article 25
Q29	**Are all ordained ministers good in matters of life and doctrine?**	Matthew 7:15 Matthew 8:25-30
A29	No. There are always both good and wicked people in the church, and sometimes wicked people will have authority to minister God's word and the sacraments.	Acts 20:29-30 2 Peter 2:1 Article 26
Q30	**What is baptism?**	Romans 6:4
A30	Baptism is a sign of Christian profession, and also a sign of regeneration. Those who are baptised are grafted into the church. The promises of forgiveness of sin, and of our adoption to be the children of God by the Holy Spirit, are visibly signed and sealed by baptism.	Galatians 3:26-28 Romans 4:11 Acts 22:16 Article 27

Q31	**Is it permissible to baptise infants?**	Genesis 17:10 Mark 10:14
A31	Certainly. The baptism of young children is in accordance with Christ's institution of the sacrament.	Acts 16:15, 33 1 Corinthians 7:14
Q32	**What is the Lord's Supper?**	1 Corinthians
A32	The Lord's Supper is a sign of Christian love, and also a sacrament of our redemption by Christ's death.	10:16-17 1 Corinthians 11:24-25 Article 28
Q33	**In what way is the body of Christ received and eaten in the Lord's Supper?**	John 6:35, 63 Acts 3:21 1 Corinthians 5:7-9 Article 28
A33	The body of Christ is given, taken, and eaten in the Lord's Supper in a spiritual manner. It is received and eaten by faith, since the physical body and blood of our Saviour Christ are in heaven and not here.	
Q34	**Can people without a living faith partake of the body of Christ in the Lord's Supper?**	John 13:27 1 Corinthians 11:27-29
A34	Certainly not. Those without a living faith do not partake of Christ, but instead bring condemnation on themselves as they eat and drink the signs of his body and blood.	Hebrews 11:6 Article 29
Q35	**Does the Lord's Supper repeat, continue, or renew Christ's sacrifice?**	1 Corinthians 11:24 Hebrews 9:28
A35	No. The Lord's Supper commemorates the one sacrifice of Christ, once made and finished upon the cross.	Hebrews 10:10-12, 14, 18 Article 31

Q36	Should the customs and liturgy of the church be the same everywhere?	1 Corinthians 14:26, 40
A36	No. It is not necessary they should be the same everywhere. They may be changed according to local custom and etiquette, so long as there is nothing which is contrary to God's word.	
Q37	Is it right for anyone to depart from the liturgy of the church by their own private judgment?	1 Timothy 5:20 Romans 16:17-18 Article 34
A37	No. People who do this should be rebuked, because it sets a precedent for others to do the same thing.	
Q38	How many orders of ministers are there in the Church of England?	Philippians 1:1 1 Timothy 3:1,10
A38	Three. For the Scriptures and the practice of the early church indicate that from the Apostles' time there have been these orders of ministers in Christ's Church: Bishops, Priests (i.e. Presbyters), and Deacons.	1 Timothy 5:19-22 Titus 1:5
Q39	What is meant by the Royal Supremacy?	2 Chronicles 24:5 Isaiah 49:23
A39	That the Queen's majesty has the chief power in this realm of England, and her other dominions, and should rule all estates and degrees committed to her charge by God, whether they are ecclesiastical or temporal.	2 Chronicles 31:2, 35:1-2 Ezra 7:27 Romans 13:1

Additional questions from the original catechism which may be of particular value for those who have been taught by the Roman Catholic Church.

Q40	**What are works of Supererogation?**	Luke 10:27
A40	These are voluntary works which go beyond God's commandments. Teaching that works of supererogation are possible is arrogant and ungodly.	Luke 17:10 Article 14
Q41	**Was the virgin Mary, or any of the apostles or prophets free from sin?**	Luke 1:47
A41	No. Christ alone was without sin. If we say we have no sin, we deceive ourselves and the truth is not in us.	1 John 1:8 Article 15
Q42	**Why should we reject Roman Catholic doctrines of purgatory, indulgences, worship, and adoration, as well as images, icons, relics, and praying to the saints?**	Luke 23:43 Isaiah 43:25 Exodus 20:4 2 Kings 18:4 Revelation 19:10
A42	Because these are human inventions which are contrary to the Scriptures.	Article 22
Q43	**May the public worship of the Church be in a language that the people do not understand, such as Latin?**	1 Corinthians 14:11, 19, 28 Article 24
A43	Certainly not. This is clearly against God's word and the practice of the early church.	
Q44	**What are the additional sacraments of the Roman Catholic Church?**	Article 25
A44	Confirmation, Penance, Holy Orders, Matrimony, Extreme Unction.	

Q45	**Why are these not counted as sacraments of the gospel?**	Article 25
A45	Some are corruptions of New Testament teaching. Others are states of life which are allowed by the Bible but do not have any visible sign or ceremony instituted by God associated with them.	
Q46	**What is meant by the sacrament of Penance and why should it be rejected?**	Mark 1:15 Luke 24:47 Acts 10:43
A46	It is claimed that, in this sacrament, sins are forgiven by the priest's absolution, together with contrition, confession, and satisfaction. However, repentance and faith are the only conditions of forgiveness which God has appointed.	Acts 13:38 Acts 20:21 Romans 3:25
Q47	**What is the doctrine of transubstantiation and why should it be rejected?**	1 Corinthians 11:26 Acts 3:21
A47	Transubstantiation is the supposed change of the substance of bread and wine in the Lord's Supper. Transubstantiation is to be rejected because it cannot be proved by Scripture, is contrary to the plain words of Scripture, goes against the nature of a sacrament, and has given rise to many superstitions.	John 6:62-63 Acts 19:26 Article 28
Q48	**Should only the minister drink the cup at the Lord's Supper?**	1 Corinthians 10:17
A48	No. The cup should not be denied to the congregation.	1 Corinthians 11:26 Article 30

Q49	**What are the sacrifices of Masses?**	Hebrews
A49	The sacrifices of Masses in which it is commonly said that the priest offers Christ, for the living and the dead, to have remission of pain or guilt, are blasphemous fables and dangerous deceits.	10:1,2,11 2 Peter 2:1-3 Article 31
Q50	**Does the Bible teach that clergy should be celibate?**	1 Corinthians 9:5
A50	No. Bishops, Priests (i.e., Presbyters), and Deacons are not commanded by God's law to make promises to remain single, or to abstain from marriage.	1 Timothy 3:2 1 Timothy 4:1-3 Article 32
Q51	**Should we acknowledge the authority of the Pope?**	2 Thessalonians 2:3-4
A51	By no means. The Bishop of Rome has no authority in England. Nor is he the Vicar of Christ or successor of Peter, but rather is believed by many to be the predicted "Man of Lawlessness," who sets himself up in God's temple, proclaiming himself to be God.	Article 37

Additional questions from the original catechism concerning other Church of England texts.

Q52	**What is the status of the Book of Homilies?**	2 Timothy 1:13
A52	The Book of Homilies contains godly and wholesome doctrine. It was necessary for the times in which it was written, and was therefore to be read in churches, diligently and distinctly, so that people could understand it.	1 Timothy 4:13

Q53	**Should we accept the Ordinal of the Church of England?**	John 20:21-23
A53	Certainly. There is nothing superstitious or ungodly in it. Anyone who is consecrated or ordained according to it should be considered rightly, orderly, and lawfully consecrated or ordained.	Luke 24:47 2 Corinthians 5:18-19

FIGHT VALIANTLY!

CONTENDING FOR THE FAITH
IN THE BIBLE AND IN THE CHURCH OF ENGLAND

What does it mean "to contend for the faith that was once for all delivered to the saints"? With so much confusion and argument in today's church, how are Christians meant to think about and react to false teaching? How can we promote the gospel lovingly in a context of opposition?

In this biblical and practical book, aimed especially at ministers and church councils, Lee Gatiss provides a unique look at the Bible's teaching on this neglected subject. As well as giving an in-depth survey of the New Testament's teaching about contending for the gospel and countering heresy, he helps us consider some of the applications of this doctrine to the Church of England today.

Includes many real-life stories of people contending for the faith, and a Bible Study Guide for individuals or groups.

"What a timely book this is! I commend Fight Valiantly wholeheartedly, both for its gospel warmth and the challenges it presents, as a wonderfully comprehensive and firm biblical basis for staying in the Church of England as we contend." **Rod Thomas, Bishop of Maidstone**

Church Society

EQUIPPING GOD'S
PEOPLE TO LIVE
GOD'S WORD